MINNESOTA
Curiosities

Help Us Keep This Guide Up to Date

Every effort has been made by the authors and editors to make this guide as accurate and useful as possible. However, many things can change after a guide is published—establishments close, phone numbers change, facilities come under new management, etc.

We would love to hear from you concerning your experiences with this guide and how you feel it could be improved and kept up to date. While we may not be able to respond to all comments and suggestions, we'll take them to heart and we'll also make certain to share them with the authors. Please send your comments and suggestions to the following address:

The Globe Pequot Press
Reader Response/Editorial Department
P.O. Box 480
Guilford, CT 06437

Or you may e-mail us at:

editorial@globe-pequot.com

Thanks for your input, and happy travels!

Curiosities Series

MINNESOTA
Curiosities

QUIRKY CHARACTERS, ROADSIDE ODDITIES & OTHER OFFBEAT STUFF

Russ Ringsak with Denise Remick

GUILFORD, CONNECTICUT

Copyright © 2003 by The Globe Pequot Press

Cover photos: Russ Ringsak and Denise Remick
Text design: Bill Brown
Layout by Deborah Nicolais
Maps created by XNR Productions Inc.; © The Globe Pequot Press

Photo credits: p. 14: Ruth Klossner; p. 16: Blue Earth Area Chamber of Commerce and Convention and Visitors Bureau; pp. 100, 101: Woodtick Inn, Cuyuna, MN; p. 106: Runestone Museum Foundation; p. 111: Longville Chamber of Commerce; p. 135: The Pilot-Independent; pp. 144, 145: Ann M. Schwartz; p. 203: Linda Studley; p. 237: Midwest Dairy Association. All other photographs by the authors.

ISBN 0-7627-2403-X

Manufactured in the United States of America
First Edition/Third Printing

To our mothers:
Ruth Baker Ringsak
and
Ruby Rydeen Remick

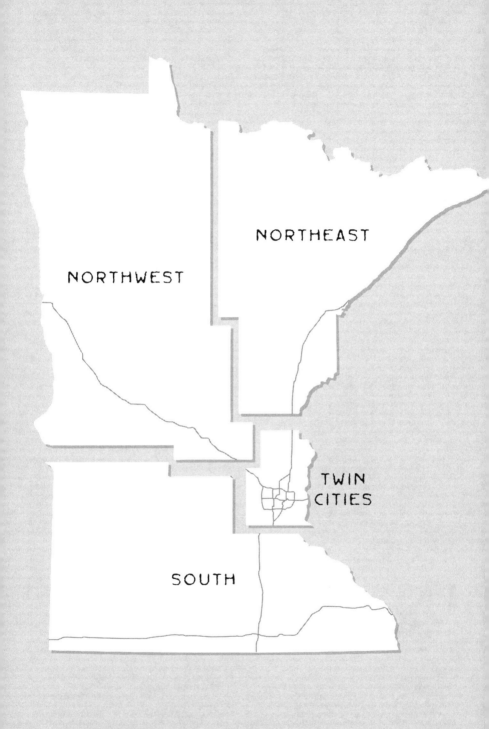

CONTENTS

ACKNOWLEDGMENTS

It requires a certain measure of confidence to offer oneself up as a subject for a book titled *Curiosities*. Some of us would be flattered to be considered *Interesting* or *Unique* or even *Different*, but a Curiosity is not that far from an Oddity in many minds, and Odd is just a step from Weird and Weird's not a goal we generally set before our children. One doesn't look at one's new baby and happily think that someday this kid might create the world's largest ball of twine, a ball so big it will take a crane to lift it.

But of course that's the whole point. Few of the contributors here set out to follow established protocol; this is a collection of people who dared to not follow the arrows painted on the pavement. These folks saw what needed doing and they did it, and where the hotel lacked cats they furnished them, and where the town lacked the spectacle of wood tick racing they invented it.

And it is to these whom we are most grateful. The bold, the innovators, the persistent, the bearers of the ridicule who carried forth and in the end achieved the huzzahs. And we thank those who helped us find them: the dedicated people at the historical societies and libraries around the state, the various chambers of commerce who assisted, and the Minnesota History Center in St. Paul.

Thanks also to the Rick Christenson family in Winona who opened the door for a couple of strangers to a number of exotic finds; to the writer Neil Haugerud, the former sheriff of Fillmore County and author of *Jailhouse Stories,* who directed us to the Hanson Museum and to Lillian's Grocery; and to Charlie Warner of the *River Valley Reader* as well as Eric Dregni, author of *Minnesota Marvels*. Thanks also to Jan Elftmann for her help in the metro area.

And a particular measure of gratitude goes to Nick and Candy Tollefson, not only for the driving and photo assistance but also for enduring the constant boring references to Das Buch. And to Wendy, Jolene, and Linda, for constructive advice and impartial critique. And to our pal Jim Cox, just on general principles.

INTRODUCTION

Minnesota, the Land of 10,000 Lakes, actually has 11,842 lakes larger than ten acres and more than 63,000 miles of rivers and streams. That's 7,762 square miles of water in all—an area of water as large as the entire state of New Jersey. (No mention of acreage is complete without some reference to New Jersey.) There are 90,000 miles of shoreline here, more than California, Florida, and Hawaii combined. It is the only state to contain the sources of three major river systems: the Red River, draining north to Hudson Bay in Canada; the St. Lawrence, draining east through the Great Lakes to the Atlantic; and the Mississippi, running south to the Gulf of Mexico. The most popular name for a Minnesota lake is Mud, but there are also lakes named Hole in the Day, Ball Club, Bad Medicine, Big Spunk, Hanging Horn, Height of Land, Ice Cracking, Pomme de Terre, Spider, Split Hand, Stalker, and Whaletail. There are Lake Lida and Lake Lizzie, and Woman Lake, Man Lake, Girl Lake, and Boy Lake. Only two counties, Rock and Olmstead, have no natural lakes at all.

It's a land of contradiction. It's the only state to vote for the Democrat presidential ticket for the last thirty years straight and it has a long history of liberal politics, but here "liberal" usually means "restrictive": Liquor stores close at 8:00 P.M. and all day Sunday. You can't buy wine or spirits in grocery stores, and it's one of only four states left where the bars close at 1:00 A.M. You can't buy a car here on Sunday and you can't buy fireworks at any time. There's plenty of public gambling—busloads of elderly hauled to casinos daily—but you can't scalp tickets to a baseball game or any other game. It's the only state to put a famous professional wrestler in its highest office and where you see faded bumper stickers that proudly read: OUR GOVERNOR CAN BEAT UP YOUR GOVERNOR. And it has an official state muffin: blueberry.

It contains the nation's oldest rock, the oldest indoor mall, and the largest shopping mall, which is also the nation's most visited attraction, a larger draw than Disney World, Yellow-

stone, and the Grand Canyon combined. However its most
famous small town, Lake Wobegon, cannot be found by anyone
because of a surveying error. Another surveying anomaly
called the Northwest Angle added a little piece of Canada to the
state, now the northernmost point in the lower forty-eight.

International Falls, called the Icebox of the Nation, is only
the fifth coldest town in Minnesota. In February 1996 the official thermometer at Embarrass broke from the cold; unofficial
thermometers read sixty-four degrees below zero. The town
bought a new thermometer that reads to seventy-five below.

Minnesota taste in sculpture runs less to nubile maidens,
nude athletes, and full-breasted robed goddesses and more to
Prairie Chickens and walleyes. There is very little in the way of
classical European sculpture here and not much of the soldier
up on a fiery steed, like they favor down south. Even serious
art here tends to run toward the whimsical, and on the less
serious side there is a frightening amount of large roadside
sculpture in the state, generally done in bright glossy colors:
74 animals and birds, 24 fish, 32 mythological creatures, 18
Indians, 8 voyageurs, 62 miscellaneous objects, and 54 adver-
tising statues; 272 in all, plus whatever has been built last
week. There are twenty-six statues here having to do with Paul
Bunyan, everything about Paul from the cradle to the grave,
including both the cradle and the grave. And a lot more,
including his ax, his ox, his girlfriend, and his CB radio. They
say his statue in Bemidji is the single most photographed
attraction in the United States.

The University of Minnesota's mascot is Goldy, the Golden
Gopher, called Golden to cover the fact it's a rodent and a pest
to farmers. It's very likely the only state wherein counties currently post a bounty on their own mascot.

Minnesota has been compared to Wisconsin by Michael Feld-
man in his funny book, *Wisconsin Curiosities,* and most of the
points he made were directly on the mark. They are certainly
more casual over there, and a couple of degrees warmer and a
couple of degrees goofier than we are, except when it comes to
their state legislators who are at least ten degrees more sensi-

ble than ours. Most of us here bear neither rancor nor envy to the state of Wisconsin, despite all their pro football championships compared to our none, our *big fat zero,* which Michael was too much of a gentleman to mention. Most of our feelings toward his state are feelings of gratitude, because they give us humor, Sunday liquor, fireworks, an extra hour after our last call, and concert tickets when we need them; best of all, they provide a nice heavy cushion between us and Illinois. They are an overstuffed pillow between ourselves and the overstressed and overcrowded masses of the East. And if their freeways are lined with billboards reading CHEESE that's no problem for us. Whatever it takes.

P.S. In the summer of 2002 the state legislators gave us permission to light sparklers and snakes; some took this as an insult and others saw it as a relaxation of tyranny. Either way, it led to an increase in the number of illegal fireworks shot off this 4th of July, especially from the forbidden launch pads on the docks of lake cabins.

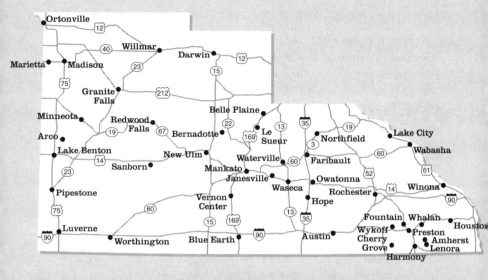

Ortonville • — 12 —
— 40 — Willmar • Darwin • — 12 —
Marietta • • Madison — 23 — — 15 —
— 75 —
Granite Falls • — 212 —
Minneota • Redwood Falls Belle Plaine • — 22 —
Arco • — 19 — — 67 — Bernadotte • Le Sueur — 13 — — 35 — — 19 — Lake City •
Lake Benton — 169 — — 3 — Northfield • Wabasha •
— 14 — New Ulm Waterville • — 60 — — 60 —
— 23 — Sanborn • Mankato Faribault • — 61 —
Pipestone • Janesville Waseca • Owatonna — 52 — Winona •
— 75 — — 60 — Vernon Center • Hope Rochester — 14 — — 90 —
Luverne • — 15 — — 169 — — 13 — — 35 — Fountain • Whalan
— 90 — Worthington • Blue Earth • — 90 — Austin Wykoff Preston • Houston
Cherry Grove • Amherst
Harmony Lenora

SOUTH

SOUTH

LILLIAN'S GROCERY
Amherst

illian's would be a grocery store like any other old grocery store clinging on past its prime if not for the stubborn feistiness of the owner, Lillian Haagenson, a small woman in her late eighties. She and her husband, Giffen, bought this store April 1, 1954. They'd farmed near Spring Grove, sold the farm, and moved to Mabel. Giffen worked as a mechanic there. Four years later he decided to buy this store and the house that went with it. The store had been closed for four years. Lillian says it was a hell of a mess and she got stuck cleaning it up. Giffen had his mechanic's shop in the back, and she ran the store.

Things were different back then, she says, and there were a lot of good folks who lived nearby, decent people who traded there regularly. Farms were smaller and she knew almost everyone who stopped by. "Most of the people I used to know have either died or moved away. The Amish and the city slickers have moved down here, bought up the farms, and moved into the woods. They don't buy much from me, not like folks did years ago."

Giffen died forty-one years ago, and the place has changed very little since. Lillian keeps the store open seven days a week, and it's generally busiest from 10:30 A.M. to 1:00 P.M.; her customers help her host the annual Christmas party and they also stage a birthday party for her. She never takes a holiday.

"Folks just expect that I'm always going to be open. Many people come down here on Sundays for a pop or a sandwich and to visit. It's usually busiest about lunchtime."

The place has been broken into seven times in the last ten years; the most recent was January 2002, when they not only took the cash register and all the cigarettes but also trashed the place. Neighbors helped clean up and local churches raised money to get Lillian back in business. There isn't a whole lot on her shelves even in the best of times. She says she never used to have trouble ". . . before all this riffraff moved into the area. It's upsetting when it happens and nothing ever happens to them when they get caught. Back in the old days when Neil Haugerud was sheriff, he would have sent them up the line. But now days the sheriff catches these hoodlums, the judge just lets them go, and they come right back and break in again. The hell with them!"

For all the problems, she's not closing the place; she enjoys it all too much.

The store sits in the valley of the South Fork of the Root River, on Fillmore County 23 in the very eastern part of the county; not only is it in Amherst, it *is* Amherst. Look for a small white-painted building behind a single gas pump, with an awning roof across the front suggesting perhaps a porch. No sign and no telephone.

STONE GAS STATION
Arco

It's a tiny town on the prairie, 101 people, and it once held a Texaco station so sensational that busloads of tourists would stop to see it. In 1949, 4,000 visitors dropped in from all over the nation.

*H. P. Pederson thought the rocks in his fields were a bonus. In
the 1930s he and his family created a stone fantasia of the
town's Texaco station.*

The building and some sculptures remain. It's not what it
used to be, but, as with a lot of us, there is enough left so you
get the idea. It was built by H. P. and Ricka Pederson and their
boys, M. M. and Vernon, a natural progression from the rock
sculptures they were already making. Farming in the early
1930s would yield rocks in every plowing, and H. P. broke
them with a sledgehammer, mortaring pieces around wire
frames to make ashtrays, lamps, flowerpots, and bookends.
There was a market for them in town.

Hugo the Ram.

In 1936 they bought the Texaco station in Arco and set out to give it the stone treatment. By then they had a lot of stone, some collected on annual trips out west, some donated by neighbors. They covered the entire exterior and built a flowing parapet on the front wall, with five open circles rising to the center, a metal Texaco star in each circle; they set a colorful stone Texaco star in a circular recess above the front door. Before they were done a fantastic stone garden flanked the station, containing an elegant stone-domed pergola, archways, a Liberty Bell shrine, a life-sized mountain goat, a dramatic Statue of Liberty, plus a Dutch windmill, a snake wrapped around a petrified log, a lighthouse, and a large Viking ship. Even its sail was stone. A stone pelican perched on one of the arches. There were also a number of miniature rock sculptures including a house and church, an entire farm, and a railroad scene complete with depot, elevator, and stone locomotive. There was stone in there from every state in the Union, of every kind and color, from quartz to jade, coral to petrified wood, and even a bit of pipestone: the stem of a stone apple, still there beneath a windowsill.

The building today is vaguely reminiscent of the Alamo, although it's occupied as a house; the metal stars are gone from inside the five circles on the parapet, and most of the garden sculptures have disappeared as well. But the goat, the Liberty Bell, the Statue of Liberty, and part of the garden wall are less than a mile away, in a park on Lake Stay.

Take County Road 19 west of Marshall for 19 miles to Route 7, then head 4 miles south to Arco.

THE DORIS GROUP

*T*wenty-three kids began first grade in Storden in 1959,
according to the official history of the Doris Group: "7
boys and 15 girls." It makes you wonder if the parents of the
other child were just not saying, or if nobody bothered to
ask. Still, the more remarkable fact about that class was
that the teacher and four of their mothers were named
Doris, as well as another teacher hired a few years later.
With six of them in the school and a few others nearby, Doris
Jean Halvorsen, the new teacher, got the idea that they
should get together for coffee.

It never quite happened, and Doris Jean passed on in
1991. But her idea still hung in the air, and finally on February 22, 1995, ten local Doris' assembled in her honor at
the Cafe in Storden. (They have concluded, over the years,
that Doris' with an apostrophe is a preferable plural to
Dorises.) The ten were Ewy, Vaupel, and Olson from West-
brook; Torkelson of Redwood Falls; Bierman and Barker of
Jeffers; Bottem of Lamberton; and Lerohl, Nelson, and Olson
of Storden. It reads like a poem.

Ten became twelve that fall in Lamberton; the next year
in Sanborn there were sixteen, and then twenty-one in Tracy,
twenty-three in Redwood Falls, twenty-four in Milroy, and
thirty-one in Wabasso. They met for the eleventh time in Bird
Island on April 26, 2000; by then they had eighty-two members. The youngest Doris, Konold, was four years old,
brought in from a nursery school; the oldest, Kolander, was
driven in from a nursing home. A banner was hung in the
dining room with the name of the event: DORIS DAY. The meeting's main order of business is to decide where to have the
next one, and Dallman of Wabasso turned to Bickman of St.
Louis Park (a Minneapolis suburb) and said: "Don't volunteer; I don't want to come to the Cities." It got a big laugh.

That fall when they met at the Redwood Falls Pizza Ranch they had become 109; the Doris Group was experiencing exponential growth. Otterson of Alexandria says, "We're an organization for people who have difficulty remembering names." And as of October 2001, there were 161 members. Doris Olson, one of the founders, says, "It's just a social event. We don't have officers or presidents or anything. I just have the list of names. We get together and everybody talks. . . . Some of these ladies, I don't know who they are. I know their name is Doris, but that's about it. Mostly we just gab a little bit and get acquainted."

And if you're wondering, Doris Day is an honorary member, even though she still hasn't been to any meetings. She did send them an autographed photo.

For information about the Doris Group, call (507) 872–5451 or write P.O. Box 183, Minneota, MN 56264.

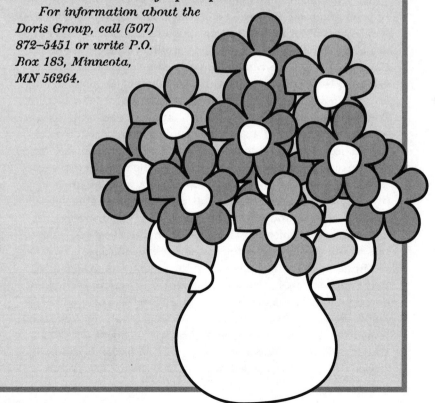

THE SPAM MUSEUM
Austin

A visitor enters the new Spam Museum beneath a wall of Spam cans, 3,390 of them, all empty but impressive nonetheless. The original Hormel Foods museum was set in a local mall in 1991, on the company's one hundredth anniversary, and contained just three items related to Spam. Even then it was such a success they had to expand it. It now covers 16,500 square feet in a refurbished K-mart building.

They had been in business for forty-five years when Jay C. Hormel proposed the idea of canning ham to his father, George A. They say George didn't think much of the idea at first but went along with it, calling the new product Hormel Spiced Ham. They wanted a catchier name and held a contest, and at the 1936 New Year's Eve party at Jay's home, Kenneth Daigneau, a guest, won a hundred dollars when he took out the five middle letters of *spiced ham* and came up with *Spam*. At the current rate of 435 cans per minute, 2003 will see the production of the 6 billionth copy. It could be argued that Mr. Daigneau will be, and in fact already is, the planet's most read writer—a man who wrote only one word, a word he himself invented and a four-letter word at that, conceived at a New Year's Eve party and now copyrighted in 111 countries: 6,000,000,000 copies in print. End to end, the twelve-ounce tins would reach around the equator fourteen times.

Minnesota isn't the state where the most Spam is consumed—that honor belongs to Hawaii—but Spam is to Minnesota what barbecue is to Texas; it's our Austin gift to the world, our flagship delicacy. Our contribution to American culture, folks, and remember: It wasn't barbecue that helped our boys win World War II. And it wasn't barbecue that carried Russian and British troops through the darkest days, either. Nossir. Old Nikita

There are those who say the Vikings discovered Spam.

Khrushchev himself said so, and Maggie Thatcher said the same thing. In fact, that wasn't barbecue in the famous Monty Python skit, and it wasn't Wisconsin cheese curds; it was good old spiced ham from Austin.

These and many other facts can be found at the new museum: One learns, for instance, that it was in 1954 that Haile Selassie I, Ethiopian emperor and father of the Rastafarian movement, visited this very plant. They say that in South Korea, Spam is considered a delicacy even to this day. And they display a letter from President Dwight D. Eisenhower, written during World War II, about the role Spam played in feeding the Allied Forces.

A 400-foot-long conveyor belt runs through portions of the museum, carrying more than 800 cans and simulating the production line: It gives visitors the chance to put on hard hats, rubber gloves, hair nets, and earplugs just like the folks who work in the real plant (Oh, Boy!!). A 5-foot replica of a Spamburger hamburger is suspended in the exit corridor, adjacent to a 17-foot burger-flipping spatula. There is a Spam Exam, an interactive quiz show that allows participants to show off their Spam knowledge. And of course there is a gift shop, selling 255 different Spam items.

Follow the signs off I–90 to the corner of North Main Street and 1937 Spam Boulevard. The museum hours are Monday through Saturday 10:00 A.M. to 5:00 P.M. and Sunday noon to 4:00 P.M. No admission fee. Call (800) LUV–SPAM for more information.

TWO-STORY OUTHOUSE
Belle Plaine

A souvenir shop called the Booger Hollow Trading Post near Dover, Arkansas, claims to have the "World's Only Double-Decker Outhouse," but it's just another claim out of Arkansas that can't stand up to scrutiny. Theirs is not only not the only

*You'd build a two-story outhouse too, if you had
eleven kids. Samuel Bowler built this three-seats-up,
three-seats-down loo in 1886.*

one—it's not even one at all: The upstairs is a fake, with a sign
that says UPSTAIRS CLOSED TIL WE FIGUR OUT PLUMMIN'. One suspects
there's no Boogers there either; but hey, it's a souvenir shop.

"America's Only 2-story Outhouse" in Gays, Illinois, *was* an
outhouse and *was* connected to apartments above a store, but
the store has been torn down and the outhouse, although
restored, stands alone and is kept locked. There is a tidy two-
story in Phelps, New York, attached to the Dr. John Q. Howe
residence, built in 1869, of brick. A two-story outhouse called
"Big John" has been spotted behind an old hotel in Nevada City,

Montana; they say there is also one in Cedar Lake, Michigan, that was once part of a railroad station.

But in Belle Plaine, Minnesota, there stands a historic and handsome white house with an outhouse on the side connected by a skyway to the second floor that, if it were given to boast, could truthfully call itself *The Only Two-story Outhouse in the Nation That Is Connected to a Real House and Isn't Made of Brick.*

It's now a serious museum and belongs to the Belle Plaine Historical Society, so if you go there for the novelty and stay for the historical interest, that's fine with them. It's called the Hooper-Bowler-Hillstrom House and was built in 1871 by a businessman from New York named Sanford Hooper. He owned a hotel, a machine shop, a foundry, and a riverboat, and had a hand in getting the first bridge across the Minnesota River built.

It was bought in 1886 by Samuel Bowler, founder of a local bank and owner of a lumberyard. He added a kitchen, an office, a bathroom with a copper-lined tub, and the now famous outhouse, three seats up and three down, with glass windows and curtains and a ventilator shaft. It's finished inside and built on a stone foundation. Theirs was a large family—eleven children, mostly girls. There is a double wall behind the ground-floor seats, as you might imagine, and the outhouse is connected to the house at the second floor only; the ground level opens to the outside.

Alfred Hillstrom bought the place about 1900; a member of this family lived here until it was sold to the historical society in 1975. It's been restored and furnished in three periods: 1850s, late Victorian, and early 1900s.

Asked if there were any funny stories about the place, a museum volunteer said, "Not that I know of; but it's never been tipped over."

The Hooper-Bowler-Hillstrom house is open to visitors from Memorial Day through Labor Day on Sunday from 1:00 P.M. to 4:00 P.M. and other times by appointment. Call (612) 873–4433 for information.

THE WORLD'S LARGEST INDOOR COW COLLECTION
Bernadotte

Rather than trying to sidestep the bad puns, it might be best to just cleanse the page quickly—run through them all and be done with it—and have no more reference to mooseums, moosic, amoosing, mooving, moôment, cowllector, cowllectable, cowabunga, cowabilia, cowzy, udderly, udderly cowzy, like no udder, and dairy-air. Done.

She grew up on a dairy farm near New Ulm, did Ruth Klossner, and was given her first pet calf at the age of four. She showed cows through her childhood, winning the 1966 Champion Holstein ribbon at the Minnesota State Fair 4-H show with a cow named Princess. She was named National Holstein Girl at a convention in Milwaukee in 1968 and picked up a B.S. degree in home economics from the University of Minnesota in 1970. In 1979 she earned a master of agriculture in animal technology and agricultural journalism at the U of M. In 1983 she began working at the *Lafayette-Nicollet Ledger* as a photographer and part-time staff writer, building a private photography business on the side. She is now the full-time editor of the *Ledger*.

And somewhere around 1980 she began to collect cows. Ruth has a record of doing well at whatever she puts her mind to, and right now she is really good at editing a newspaper and accumulating cows; at this writing she has 9,162 cows. She has her own version of the fabled King Ranch in Texas, which once covered nine counties, only without the heat and the dust and the flies.

When you come in and sign the guest book and you reach for a cow candy in the cow dish it moos at you, and from there on it just gets better. Cows on and of everything: cow toys,

More cows in here than in a Spaghetti Western.

napkin holders, pictures, butter dishes, statuary small medium and large, a cow rocking chair, wooden wall hangings, alarm clocks, Chicago cows, New York cows, watches, books, caps, shirts, hand towels, greeting cards, belt buckles, pencils, ties, banks, jewelry, COW beauty soap from Japan; cow booby traps, including one that moos at you when you open the refrigerator door, and cow cookie jars that do the same. Cow refrigerator magnets, key chains, calendars, salt and pepper shakers, and butter dishes. International cows from Russia, Poland, Switzer-

land, Denmark, Belgium, and Norway, and a sixteen-pound
cast-iron cow from Japan; cows rare and elegant and cows common and ordinary. A room called the shirt shack with the walls
covered with cow T-shirts, where she can grab a shirt to wear
right off the display. Mechanized cows, cow mailboxes, cow
nativity figures, and even a cow carved from a dried cowpie. A
resurrection, of sorts.

Visitors are welcome to the world's largest cow museum,
where she is up to the eyeballs in cows and, apparently, would-
n't have it udderwise.

The museum is located in Bernadotte on County Road 10
and County Road 1 northeast of New Ulm. For a tour of the
Ruth's Cow Collector's Mooseum, write or call Ruth Klossner,
Rural Route 1, Box 132B, Lafayette 56054; (507) 228–8573.

JOLLY GREEN GIANT
Blue Earth

Not surprisingly, the biggest piece of roadside art in the state
is a smiley guy in a skimpy green outfit, with pointy green
shoes and his hands on his hips and looking satisfied at what
he sees. Which of course is mostly green fields in summer and
miles of snow in winter, and somewhat of a mess in between.

He's 55 feet tall and was built just in time to oversee the
completion of Interstate 90 on September 24, 1978, the last
piece of it between the coasts; sort of like the driving of the
golden spike when the railroads joined but at a lower level of
excitement. They used imported yellow paint brushed on the
centerline; the governor, Miss Minnesota, and Miss America
were on hand for it, and the giant has been grinning ever
since. Ho ho ho.

What's big and jolly and green all over? We'll give you one guess.

Blue Earth is also the birthplace of the ice cream sandwich, but that's been overshadowed by the big fellow. Had it happened in some other town, a town that didn't already have a Jolly Green Giant, they might have put up a big ice cream sandwich statue.

If you turn south onto U.S. Highway 169 from I–90 at Blue Earth . . . as they say, you can't miss it.

WORLD'S LARGEST BALL OF TWINE
Darwin

One thinks of a ball of twine as a comfort, fitting nicely into the hand and a good thing to have around if one is recycling cardboard boxes. To farmers it's much more, especially those who deal with cattle and hay, but no matter one's pursuits it seems at home in the barn, in the garage, or in a kitchen drawer. One buys it at a certain size and over time it loses mass, like stars do, and eventually it becomes a black hole and one goes to buy another.

In Darwin a fellow named Francis A. Johnson had a ball of twine that just kept getting bigger, in direct contradiction to prevailing Ball of Twine theories, until it found itself in the *Guinness Book of World Records* and a subject of a song by Weird Al Yankovic. It began in 1950 when he wrapped two fingers with twine and then just kept wrapping, four hours a day, until it got so big he had to move it with railroad jacks to keep the growth circular; ultimately he had it raised off the ground with a crane so he could work all sides.

It grew in his yard for thirty-nine years, until Francis died in 1989 and left it to the city of Darwin. They moved it a block south to the base of the water tower, where it sits inside its own Plexiglas gazebo in the Twine Ball Compound, which naturally includes a souvenir shop. It's 40 feet around, more than 12 feet in diameter, and weighs 17,400 pounds. It's the size of an asteroid; we're glad it grew here and didn't fall out of the sky. It abuses the notion of what a ball is, especially a ball of twine. Which of course is the whole point.

Now, there are other twine balls around that claim to be larger, but some of those have plastic twine in them—an abomination to the purist—and aren't nearly as heavy; and the main thing they aren't is that they aren't wrapped by one person. None of them. They are all team efforts, which really isn't the same thing at all.

And if any one man was destined to create the World's Largest Ball of Twine Rolled by One Man, it was probably Francis. He had the initial pressure of being the son of someone famous—U.S. senator Magnus Johnson—and on top of that was a compulsive collector; he claimed to have 5,000 pencils, 200 feed caps, and an unknown large number of wooden ice cream containers. The twine caught the public's imagination, however, and catapulted him into the fame he enjoyed, which is today greater even than that of his father the senator.

Darwin celebrates "Twine Ball Days" on the second Saturday in August, just in time to catch motorcycle traffic returning from the big Sturgis Rally in South Dakota. You don't want to miss it.

The Ball of Twine Museum is on County Road 14, which runs south out of Darwin off U.S. Highway 12. For information call (320) 693-6651 or visit www.geocities.com/hollywood/theater/5805.

SINKHOLE CAPITAL OF THE USA
Fountain

L ooking at a black-and-white aerial photograph of Fountain, population 315, one immediately assumes the paper has been used for target practice with a 12-gauge shotgun. It's hard to count exactly how many, but within a mile and a half of the town there look to be about 400 hits.

These are not potholes, which form in rock at the base of waterfalls or where sand and gravel are swirled in a stream, but are karst sinks, formed when underground limestone collapses from the action of rainwater; the underlying stone drops, and the topsoil drops with it. (To most Minnesotans, potholes happen when ice and salt freeze in the road surface and kick up huge shards of pavement, leaving axle-cracking craters big enough to homestead.)

There are about 5,750 karst sinks in Fillmore County, varying in size from 30 to 150 feet across; the deepest go down 30 feet, and in winter kids slide down the sides. They can't do this in all sinks, though, because most have a tree growing right smack in the center. Others have steep walls. This is also the reason you can drive all the way through Fillmore County and not see a single sinkhole; you look out in a wheat field and think you're seeing 20-foot trees sitting out there, but they are actually crowns of 40-foot trees in 20-foot holes.

People used to throw their garbage in the steep ones, until it became obvious the garbage was soaking down there at the same level as a lot of wells and was feeding springs to boot. So they don't use 'em for landfills anymore. Instead the town of Fountain did what most places do when they have some less-than-useful aberration: turned them into a tourist attraction. It worked on us.

There is a sinkhole at the entrance to the city, near the WELCOME sign, and a viewing platform not far away. The town brochure mentions other attractions: "The warm and friendly people of Fountain welcome you! The small town atmosphere is perfect for a pleasant and relaxing visit. . . ." And so forth. The Proud Sponsors of the brochure like to use mottoes: A cafe is "Open 7 Days"; a car wash says, "A Clean Car is a Happy Car"; and Willie's Grocery and Locker says, "Where You Meat Your Friends."

Fountain is located south of Rochester on U.S. Highway 52. You can see sinkholes from almost any road in the county, especially on County Road 80 between Wykoff and Fountain.

PIETENPOL AIR CAMPER

In 1924, three years before Lindbergh crossed the Atlantic, a man named Bernard Pietenpol in Cherry Grove built an airplane powered by an engine from a Model T Ford; he knew how to build one before he knew how to fly. He managed the takeoff but not the landing and ended up nosediving into a field, flopping the plane forward onto its back—the forward-roll maneuver that aviation instructors now encourage pilots to avoid. In 1928 he did successfully build and fly an aircraft that came to be known, through a journalist's remark, as the Air Camper, a design still being built today. You can order plans for it, and with a minimum of tools and a little welding you can be airborne for a few thousand dollars. They've been built now for seventy-three years, and it'd be hard to argue with the claim that this is the most successful airplane design in history.

The Air Camper has an open cockpit and weighs forty-three pounds less than a Harley Davidson Fat Boy (another open cockpit design); although it's not quite as fast as the Harley, it doesn't have to deal with road construction and carries the same number of passengers. Bernard's first one was a single-seater that had a frame built of wood from the local lumberyard, covered with bedsheet material painted with clear varnish. The landing gear was built from gas pipe and motorcycle wheels, the fittings were made at a blacksmith shop, and the engine was a water-cooled Ace four-cylinder, turning a propeller hand-carved from black walnut. It was flown fifty hours in its first two months.

Bernard made some changes in the landing gear and began using Ford Model A engines for power. The final two-seater design and drawings were finished in 1934 and haven't changed since. A factory was set up in Cherry Grove and another in Wykoff, and airplane kits were shipped from both places until World War II broke out in 1941, when Bernard officially became an aviation instructor. Over the years other engines have been used: Ford V8, Velie, Kinner, Lycoming, Franklin, Continental; when the Chevy Corvair was introduced in 1960, Bernard built an Air Camper to use its air-cooled engine. It was lighter and smoother and put out more power with less fuel. Modified plans are available for mounting various engines. The baggage compartment is still where it's always been: The passenger climbs in and you put the luggage in their lap.

Bernard's son and his grandson are both still in the home-built aircraft business. The garage where it all started was also hand-built, originally as a place to repair Ford Model Ts; the building is now on the National Register of Historic Places. Different times now; hard to picture some guy designing a moon rocket that you could build yourself out of stuff from your hardware store. Hard even to imagine going out in your yard and building a garage that would someday end up as a National Historic Place.

The Pietenpol Scout 1932 plane can be seen at the Fillmore County Historical Center in Fountain. Call (507) 451–2904 for information.

WORLD'S OLDEST ROCK
Granite Falls

It's not something you'd expect to find in soybean country, but in the parking lot of the Yellow Medicine County Historical Museum just south of downtown Granite Falls, there is a sign that says WORLD'S OLDEST ROCK. There's a lichen-covered outcropping there of Morton gneiss (pronounce it nice) that's 3.6 billion years old. It's hard as rock; they'll let you sit right on it, even though it's that old.

The planet itself is 4.5 billion years old; most rock that reached the crust in the early eons has long crumbled into dust, or been drawn back down into the mantle. But the stone in this outcropping has been through an incredible series of geologic events, the most recent one when Lake Agassiz—a huge glacial lake that is now the Red River Valley—burst through a natural earth berm on its lower end and cut a trench through southern Minnesota. It was 180 feet deep in some places and took off an enormous amount of soil, revealing the shiny edge of solid rock that can be seen, here and there, for 60 miles along the Minnesota River; veteran rock from the Archean eon, when the earth's crust and oceans were formed. Geologists from around the world come here to visit it.

Now, 3,600,000,000 years is what they call "deep time"; time unimaginable. If a grown male spreads his arms and stretches his fingers out as far as they can reach, and if that distance, fingernail tip to fingernail tip, represents the age of this rock, then one firm stroke of an ordinary nail file would scratch off all of human experience, all the way back to before the beginnings of the Neanderthals. Two hundred thousand years, gone in one quick scratch.

It's impossible to grasp even the time in that scratch; getting a grip on the age of this rock is right up there with trying

A rock older than dirt.

to understand the distance across the Milky Way. For those of us who can't even remember the last Super Bowl, a more useful mental exercise might be to just sit on the rock and try to imagine the next birthday coming up that we'll get in trouble for if we forget.

The Yellow Medicine County Historical Museum is at the convergence of Minnesota Highways 23 and 67 and U.S. Highway 212.

NIAGARA CAVE
Harmony

Niagara cave has all the ingredients of a good road stop: history, mystery, fossils, a granddaddy stalactite, a wishing well, sunflower coral, a wedding chapel, and a 60-foot-high underground waterfall.

In 1941 a touring Al Capone and his wife stopped in; this of course was after his Alcatraz tour. But it was popular with the local population before the celebrities discovered it. There have been hundreds of weddings down there, too—enough that older people coming to the place are often couples who were married there in the 1950s. A catered prom dinner was once held in the cave.

It's a fissure cave, as opposed to the tunnel type, meaning that it consists of interconnected undergound cracks in a stone plate, if you can call a room 130 feet tall with a creek and a waterfall running through it a "crack." The granddaddy stalactite is 8 feet long and is in a big room 225 feet below the surface, with a bunch of his relatives. The sunflower coral is actually 350-million-year-old algae from the time of the first insects—the late Devonian epoch, when the Appalachians were formed and everything was all one continent. The various fossils are older yet, dating back 450 million years, to a time before life grew on the land. The limestone plate itself is 500,000 years old and was at one time situated on the equator.

The cave was discovered in 1924 by farm boys looking for three missing pigs, according to the story. They found a narrow sinkhole, peered in, and heard squealing way down below; professionals went down and found the pigs and a whole lot more. Must have been quite an experience for those boys; they were probably telling the story the rest of their lives, to anyone who would listen. When word got out the three cavers formed a partnership and leased the place, and by 1934 pathways had been built and lighted for the tourist trade. The present owner, Mark Bishop, is a caver himself—a term now favored over *spelunker*—and has explored most of the network not open to the public; it extends well past the 1-mile underground tour.

It is an amazing place. In the last room you look way down and see the creek disappear into a sheer wall. It travels in primeval darkness south through a few miles of rock to the river bluffs, where it reappears as two natural clear-water springs, the Hawkeye and Odessa Springs, along the Upper Iowa River, which runs east into the muddy reality of the Mississippi.

Niagara Cave is located 2 miles south of Harmony on Minnesota Highway 139, then 2 miles west on Niagara Cave Road; it's 1 mile north of the Minnesota-Iowa border on MN 139. The cave is open daily from May through September, 9:30 A.M. to 5:30 P.M.; April and October it is open weekends only. For more information call (507) 886–6606 or write Niagara Cave, P.O. Box 444, Harmony, MN 55939.

DARDEVLE ART
Hope

When Jim and Millie Stockwell's grand old front-yard white ash died in 1997, they had the Knutson Brothers leave the main trunk, 12 feet tall and straight up. Neighbors asked why they left such a tall stump, and they said, "Well, just wait a while. It'll change."

They had hired chain-saw sculptor Dale Brooks to carve it into a huge northern pike dancing on its tail, a big Dardevle

A front yard depiction of a typical scene on a Minnesota lake.

lure hooked into its lower lip; the line leads to a fisherman standing on the roof of their house. Fishing nearby is a man in a flat-stern canoe with a 1938 Johnson Sea Horse motor; the submerged part of the motor is not really buried, Jim says, but just cut off, so if anyone takes that motor they won't be getting much. Ducks float in the cattails around the canoe, and the angler has caught a basketful of ordinary-sized fish. The monster erupts 10 feet from his boat.

At night the line from the Dardevle to the house is lit up, as well as the big northern's eyes and the bucket of fish. The eyes are convincing round mirrors with the backing scraped off the centers.

While you are in Hope you might also check out the Hope Creamery, a 1950s-style one-man butter-making operation that produces a two or three batches a week, butter made the way it should be made and all of it tasting exactly like butter tasted when you were a kid—"fresh as country air." It's for sale at the Krause Service Station there in town—an interesting place in itself—and also available at selected grocery stores around the Twin Cities.

From Interstate 35 south of Owatonna, take County Road 4 west to Hope; the fish is on the right side of the road at the north end of town. The Hope Creamery is downtown on the main drag.

CODY THE BUFFALO
Houston

There is a vivid scene in the film *Dances with Wolves* wherein the most immense bison you've ever imagined has an Indian spear driven clean through him and is running with both ends sticking out, like shish kebab on the hoof. That bison is now back home at the Money Creek Buffalo Ranch, none the worse for experience—in fact better off. His name is Cody, and he weighs a ton and then some. He's only fourteen years old and is enjoying a satisfying career as a movie star and local celebrity.

Disney wanted Cody bad. They were offering a seven-digit number and had plans for him at the Wild West show in their new Euro Disney theme park in France but his owner, Mike Fogel, said no way, not at any price.

He's featured in another movie, *Radio Flyer,* he and Tom Hanks, John Heard, and Ben Johnson; Hollywood paid the boy $200,000 for that one. He has appeared at countless fairs,

Some bison will do anything for a buck.

parades, and school events, been center stage at the Mall of America, and achieved equal billing with the Energizer Bunny in a television commercial. He's been on *Newton's Apple* and featured in *National Geographic* and *People* magazine; was in a Subway commercial for Buffalo Chicken Sub sandwiches.

He is living a good life there on the ranch, surrounded by exotics from around the world: Nilgai antelope from India, with two dots on their faces and stripes on their ankles; wild Russian hogs from the Black Forest with hair on their backs; Mouflon sheep from France, peacocks from China, pygmy goats, miniature and full-sized horses, and, for balance, some plain old Minnesota white-tailed deer.

Buffalo Gal is the name of the company. They not only book Cody tours but also offer buffalo on the hoof or in the package: heifers, bull calves, breeding bulls, cows, natural free-range rib eyes, sirloin, sausage, and filet mignon; buffalo wool, robes, bleached buffalo skulls, painted shoulder blades, beaded pipe-stone leather necklaces, and a lot more. Buffalo Gal's motto is "Everything from Conception to Consumption."

They offer breakfast and lunch tours of the Money Creek Buffalo Ranch as well as free service for even a hard-core vege-tarian: You can go to the ranch and have your picture taken with Cody. You can't do that in France, and we in Minnesota are grateful.

You can buy almost anything related to the critters from buffalogal.com, or you can call (507) 896–2345 and talk directly to Mike himself. Money Creek Buffalo Ranch is on County Road 76 north of Houston, south off I–90.

Star quality pays off.

TILT-A-WHIRL

*Y*ou could ride a Tilt-A-Whirl 100,000 times in a row, if the carnival were in town long enough, and every single ride would be different. This was not the exact goal that woodworker Herbert W. Sellner set out to achieve when he invented and built the machine in 1926, but mathematicians using computers and the latest Chaos Theory formulae have taken it upon themselves to analyze what it takes to make fun fun, and they've proven that unpredictability is a big part of it.

Herbert had already pioneered breathtaking fun in 1923 when he invented the Water Toboggan Slide, a fabulous large wooden structure built out over the water where you would climb the ladder with your sled and then slide down at a high rate of speed and go zinging along the water for 100 feet or so; they were "installed at beaches around the world."

The first Tilt-A-Whirl was operated at an amusement park in White Bear Lake, Minnesota. It was built mainly of wood and had nine swinging cars, each pivoting on its own platform about its own center; the cars rotate together over a roller-coaster track, causing each one to swing in different ways. As the mathematicians put it: "When the motion is chaotic . . . the resulting plot, known as a Pinker section, shows points scattered across the plane . . . the system is constantly shifting from one unstable periodic motion to another, giving the appearance of great irregularity . . . the movements of an individual car resemble those of a friction-impaired pendulum hanging from a support that is both

rotating and being rocked back and forth while the pendulum swings." *Easy for them to say.*

At any rate, the Tilt-A-Whirl was an instant hit, with hundreds sold to parks and carnival operators across the United States. The Sellner Manufacturing Company is still in Faribault, where it began, and is still in the hands of the family; the president is Erin Sellner Ward, fun-loving Herbert W.'s great-granddaughter. Her husband is vice president and general manager. They sell other rides the company has designed, but the Tilt-A-Whirl is still the biggest seller. It has changed somewhat, now having seven cars instead of nine and being built of steel, aluminum, and fiberglass, but it is still rugged, reliable, easy to assemble, and very popular. Lately the company has been getting requests from people who want one in their own backyard; a new status symbol, apparently, in some level of our amazing society.

It is a fun ride for the operator, who has control of the overall rotating speed. He or she can pick out one car and, by just a slight acceleration at precisely the right second, can fling that car into a high-speed spin. Once they master that, some operators move up to the Advanced Hysteria Level in which they can accelerate two cars at once. And since each car carries different weight in different positions, no two ever behave quite the same. The added benefit to the operator of maximizing the spin velocity—above the extra squealing—is that it means more change spills out of riders' pockets.

Physicist Richard L. Klutz of the National Institute of Standards and Technology says: "Ride designers have been fairly adept at finding chaos without appreciating the mathematics underpinning what they're doing."

W I N D   F A R M S
L a k e   B e n t o n

They're big and there are a lot of them. It's an awesome sight. They're Zond Z-750 wind towers and they ride Buffalo Ridge in Lincoln County. They reach 257 feet up, weigh 100 tons, and are anchored in 420 tons of reinforced concrete. They're made in the USA and they've got gearboxes, heaters, induction generators, 165-foot propellers, and computer control. Each kicks out enough juice for 250 homes, even homes with dishwashers and teenagers.

They don't have that western-movie nostalgic look of the old windmills, with all the vanes close together, up on that graceful wooden tower. With the single tube and the big three-blade prop, these things look whimsical, like gigantic children's toys stuck out in the field; tractors look like miniatures beneath them. But Buffalo Ridge is a natural home for them; its real name is the Bemis moraine, a long pile of rock and debris left at the farthest reach of the last glacier, the highest place in southwestern Minnesota and right in the path of the prevailing prairie wind.

The town of Lake Benton calls itself the Windpower Capital of the Midwest, sitting in the middle of two big groups of towers—354 in all, and a lot more to come. Plans are afoot to triple the output of the farms by 2015, because they look dramatic and they make environmentalists smile.

The windmills stand along U.S. Highway 75, primarily between Pipestone and Ivanhoe.

Lake Benton calls itself the Windpower Capital of the Midwest, and for good reason. The town sits in the middle of 354 wind towers.

THE BIRTH OF WATERSKIING

*I*n 1922 the tomb of Tutankhamen was discovered in Egypt, the USSR was formed, the BBC began broadcasting in England, and Mussolini came to power in Italy; here in the United States, Prohibition had been in effect for two years and we were about ready to party, and at that critical juncture in history a reckless eighteen-year-old kid from Lake City, Minnesota, invented waterskiing. It didn't exactly hurl us into the Roaring Twenties, but it did nothing to hold us back, either.

His name was Ralph Samuelson. His youth was spent as a Huck Finn river rat; he dived for clams in the 30-mile-long and 3-mile-wide spot in the Mississippi known as Lake Pepin, two blocks from his home. They were sold to a now long-gone factory in town that made them into shell buttons.

He tried it first with snow skis. After he was dragged like a boulder behind his brother's twenty-four-horsepower boat for a couple of hours, he decided they weren't wide enough. Barrel staves didn't have enough curl, and he was dragged for another few hours. He went to a lumberyard and bought two 8-foot pine boards, 9 inches wide. He boiled the front ends in water and clamped them around a curved surface to curl the tips. After two more days of being dragged around the lake in front of the whole town, he got the idea of keeping the tips up when his brother hit the power, and on July 2, the last day before his nineteenth birthday, he rose upright out of the water, driving his friends on the shore wild. He had to zigzag to stay up because the boat could only reach 20 miles an hour.

He made better skis and found more powerful boats, up to one with a propeller and an airplane engine that could hit 50. He built a greased ski jump and would amaze vacationers by jumping 60 feet and landing upright. He went from the boat to a World War I Curtis-Wright flying boat, and sometimes at 80 miles an hour it'd get airborne in spite of itself and carry him 20 feet above the water. The first time he lost a ski he invented slalom skiing right there. He invented barefoot skiing when he lost both of them. The young man never got hurt doing this.

And he never made any money at it, either. Bought a yellow roadster and toured the country and did sensational shows from Florida to Detroit, but he'd only take enough to pay his expenses. His son Jon later said, "That was Americana in those days. The whole country was filled with people who were unique and didn't invent something to become famous and rich, but just to try something new."

He injured his back and wrist in an accident unrelated to waterskiing and eventually moved back to Minnesota, to Mazeppa, and the nation forgot about him. He became a success at raising turkeys and was married in the late 1940s to a woman named Hazel, who said, "When I married Ralph, I didn't know anything about his death-defying waterskiing. But I knew we were defying something to raise turkeys."

He was rediscovered in the mid-1960s and recognized for what he'd done, and for the last ten years of his life rode in parades and made speeches on behalf of the state. In 1977 Ralph was invited to Winter Haven, Florida, for groundbreaking ceremonies at the Water Ski Hall of Fame, where he was a charter member. Hazel said later: "He shouldn't have gone—we wanted him to go back to the Mayo Clinic—but it was important to him to make that trip. As soon as he got home, he passed away."

Another Lake City resident, Dennis Francis, traveled the entire navigable length of the Mississippi on water skis in the summer of 1973. It was 1,842 miles; his expenses were $17,000. He started on July 3, Ralph's birthday, and reached the Gulf of Mexico thirteen days later, where, according to a newspaper account, "Some 20 dolphins formed a welcoming party." At $9.32 a mile, they should have brought champagne.

THE HANSON WILDLIFE MUSEUM
Lenora

It's like reviewing a hidden Metropolitan Museum of Art, this place; more than a person can comprehend in one dose. Bruce Hanson began collecting as a kid, when he was walking behind his father's plow and saw an Indian spearhead disappear beneath the soil. He couldn't find it and says he's had his eyes on the ground ever since.

The museum, at the end of a driveway lined with bowling balls, is a campus of eighteen buildings in hilly country, most of them small farm structures built for raising poultry and the like. They remind you of oysters, funky and rough on the outside and quite something else inside. Like medieval churches in Mexico. They contain amazing collections from around the world; wildlife has been Bruce's main interest, but there is a building full of antique cast-iron kitchen utensils and Avon products; a building featuring small metal sculptures, and one of natural wood oddities, burls and Florida knees, ginseng roots, mushrooms, and so forth; and yet another of beautiful wood carvings from artists far and wide. He gathers these pieces at auctions, estate sales, and junkyards, through word of mouth, and by pure chance.

A building contains a jaw-dropping collection of horns and antlers, from Cape buffalo to roe deer from the Black Forest and including the not-as-rare-as-you-might-think jackalope, a half-jackrabbit half-antelope critter commonly seen in saloons in the American West. Another shed holds a fantastic collection of knives like you never quite imagined knives could be. Yet another is full of axes and hand tools, including an ax that looks like it was designed for beheadings but was actually used to trim logs for house construction. A separate building contains 1,400 wrenches, plus gripping tools of all types.

Nothing says "welcome" like a collection of animal skulls.

There's a collection of wild animal pelts, including one of the now extinct civet cat and also featuring marmot, mink, weasel, marten, Alaskan wolverine, Canadian bobcat, and fox of many breeds—an inventory of the wild fauna of North America. Another little building contains the fantastic seashells of the world, thousands of them, causing visitors to ooh and aah uncontrollably. Bruce has the fossil of a giant squid, found on his own land.

He has the ordinary as well as the exotic: figurines, license plates, horseshoe collections. A thousand bottles and cans take you through the history of American patent medicine and beer, and although Mr. Hanson has never been a beer drinker, he has 500 brands of it on display, including the famous J. R. Ewing and Gilly's brands from Texas and Billy Beer from the ex-president's brother. (Ne'er-do-well relatives seem to be a common affliction of Democrat presidents.)

He's farmed this land since taking over from his dad, sheared sheep—5,000 in one year—and worked for a while for a well-known fur buyer, once skinning a hundred raccoons in a single night; he's also hunted ginseng, especially back when it was plentiful and when the searchers would only take a portion and leave the rest to grow. He says it was not uncommon for him to have a hundred pounds of it dried for sale at the end of the season; asked if used it himself, he replies: "No. . . . It ain't good for nothin'." He's worked as a logger, selling timber from the property, and as a taxidermist.

The security system consists mainly of nine dogs, penned in the day and loose at night, and an alert owner; you aren't sure what other measures are in place, but the single robbery attempt against him was foiled quickly and he hasn't been bothered since.

Schoolkids are brought here on field trips, although, he says, the next-door neighbors have never been through the place. They just don't know what they're missing.

The Hanson Wildlife Museum is on County Road 24, 1½ miles west of Lenora. Lenora itself is not easy to find, but it's about 7 miles east and 2 miles north of Harmony, down there close to the Iowa line.

B LUE M OUND M YSTERY
L u v e r n e

In southwestern Minnesota near the South Dakota border there is a large outcropping of Sioux quartzite rock—rock formed at the bottom of a sea a billion and a half years ago—called the Blue Mound and now part of the Blue Mound State Park. One side of the formation drops off into cliffs that may or may not have been the site of Plains Indian buffalo jumps—a discussion one would think would be easy to settle just on the evidence.

A more interesting mystery sits not far away: a line of rocks a quarter mile long lying on an east–west azimuth. Twice a year—at the spring and fall equinoxes—the sun rises directly at the east end of this line and sets on the west end of it, meaning that twice a year at least a dozen people climb the mound and sit and wait for dawn. The land is fairly quiet most of the rest of the time; it contains a goodly stand of big bluestem grasses, which can grow an inch a day and get to 7 feet tall, and a herd of bison numbering forty-five animals. They have reintroduced a hundred different native wildflowers to the park, and there are patches of prickly pear cactus on some of the shallow soils on the rock; in late June and early July, they bloom yellow.

There has been no agreement as to who built the line of rocks, though it's accepted that they have been in place for many centuries. Some like to think they were set by white men from a time even earlier than the Norsemen's arrival; others say they were set in place by ancient peoples who predated the known Indian tribes, and may be related to other celestial references in stone scattered around the American West and in Canada. Nothing fires the imagination like big rocks with unknown histories.

Blue Mound State Park is 2 miles north of Luverne on U.S. Highway 75, the King of Trails.

THE MYSTERY BOY

In the small town of Janesville there is a roadside park with a small memorial containing a time capsule. It's a sweet little place, worth stopping for, but the icon for which the town is famous is nothing as grand as that; it's just a life-sized figure in a high gabled attic window of a two-story frame house by U.S. Highway 14.

A young boy, maybe five, stands behind the glass. He has a round face, his head tilted to the right and down, looking to the street as if expecting someone. He has chubby cheeks and far-spread eyes; a short nose. There is an expression of interest about the mouth. He's wearing a jacket or shirt with a collar, and has what appears to be a bird on his head. But it could be a hat.

For Sale: Three-bedroom, two-bath house; small child in attic.

If you ask a teenage girl in Winona if she knows of any unusual places around there, she might say, "Well, there's that boy in the window in Janesville," and her mother will say, "Don't tell 'em about that. That's nothing they'd be interested in." But of course we would, and so are a lot of people. He is a compelling figure up there; not unlike the statue of the woman in the Savannah harbor, looking out to sea, waiting for a certain sailor whom we all know isn't coming back.

Motorists stop and take pictures. At least once a week a stranger will ask about it, and years ago someone called the county nurse and reported a boy held captive. The house has been in the family for a hundred years, but no one is quite sure when the boy first appeared in the window. The owner, Ward Wendt, is friendly and will show you an interesting parlor full of antiques, but he has little to say about the mystery boy.

So without a ready-made legend from the household itself, people have made up their own. Some say the clothes are never changed; others say they're changed daily. Some say there was a terrible tragedy, and others claim he's actually not a boy at all but some creature in disguise, one capable of putting curses on people. Some say there is a camera hidden up there. There are dozens of versions, which become more intense around Halloween.

A great favor this boy has done for his neighbors, to loosen so many imaginations. And to show us what can be done with a simple figure and a long and sustained silence.

Janesville sits on US 14 about 9 miles east of Mankato. You can see the Mystery Boy on the highway a block before the main street in town.

LUTEFISK AND OUTHOUSE RACES
Madison

The World's Largest Codfish sits in J. F. Jacobson Park on a base that reads:

MADISON MN
LUTEFISK CAPITAL
USA

It was commissioned in 1982 when two members of the city council proposed they give themselves that title because they had been holding lutefisk celebrations in town for a long time. They probably didn't need to add that the title was vacant, that it had always been vacant, and that it was unlikely anyone else would ever want it, *lutefisk* being the Norwegian word for gelatinous remains of codfish slabs packed in lye in wooden barrels to withstand the rigors of long trips in sailing ships. It's often slimy and doesn't smell all that great, but boiled and buttered it's really not that bad. To a Scandinavian, anything boiled and buttered can be pretty decent.

The statue was finished in 1983 and turned out real nice; 25 feet long, fiberglass, finished in bright acrylics. It has ten fins and a fat belly, and a wide-awake fish-eye openmouthed look of surprise and wonderment. It was named Lou T. Fisk and in 1984 was hauled to other places named Madison, as in Wisconsin, Ohio, New Jersey, and Connecticut, with a stop at Madison Avenue in New York on the way. This put the town on the map, however briefly, when the story was picked up by CBS-TV, NBC-TV, the *Wall Street Journal,* the *New York Times,* the *Chicago Tribune,* and the *Christian Science Monitor.*

You can tune a piano, but you can't tune a cod.

On November 7, 2002, they will kick off their thirtieth annual Norsefest celebration, which in 2001 again drew national notice with a crew from Charles Osgood's CBS *Sunday Morning* show. Look for ethnic costumes, dumplings and ham, krumkake, rommegrot, lefse, and lutefisk. And outhouse races, possibly less dramatic than NASCAR racing; there's just one outhouse, it's open, with a roof and a toilet seat. It's pushed around a pylon-marked timed course, three to a team, and it features the so-called Norwegian steering—turn right, go left. And it's very touchy, so people get flustered and run into curbs and pylons. It makes for amusing racing.

And for all the other excitement, the highlight of the Norse-fest Evening of Entertainment, November 9, is the Lutefisk Eating Contest; native son Jerry Osteraas is the longtime and current title holder as this book goes to press, but his brother-in-law, Duane Schuette of Plato, took the crown in 1999 and 2000; Jerry won it back in 2001. It has the makings of a Muhammad Ali–Joe Frazier rematch. It's not an event for the faint of heart; the winner generally needs to put down about eight pounds of lutefisk. Many of us get queasy just looking at a single serving.

For Madison information call the chamber of commerce at (320) 598-7373.

SALT LAKE
Marietta

There's a 250-acre lake on a country road in Lac Qui Parle County near the South Dakota border, surrounded by grasslands and open country. The only structure visible is a platform, accessible from a gravel parking lot, and a sign remembering Mrs. C. E. Peterson. It is the most alkaline body of water between the Atlantic Ocean and Great Salt Lake.

Goodman Larson lived next door to Mrs. Peterson, as a boy in neighboring Madison in the 1930s; she was a pharmacist and one of the few birders in that part of the country in those days. She'd take him along to help band birds, and she'd often spot unusual species at the lake, ocean birds and birds like Marbled Godwits, Snowy Egrets, Cattle Egrets, Eared Grebes, as well as Horned and Western Grebes. She'd report these to Dr. Roberts, then the curator of the Museum of Natural History at the University of Minnesota, and he'd occasionally question her accuracy; these are not Minnesota birds. "So . . . she would catch one in a trap and then, while she's a lovely lady, to prove that she was right, she'd squeeze it until it died and she'd send it to him."

It was through her early interest that this lake was preserved; she personally banded thousands of birds, more than anyone ever had at the time, and she brought the place to the attention of naturalists who would later rescue it from becoming a dumping ground for farm machinery and general junk—a status it was well on the way to acquiring. It is now a major station for the MOU, the Minnesota Ornithological Union, drawing birders worldwide to see migrating avocets and Sandhill Cranes; Tundra Swans, Snow Geese, and Red-necked and Wilson's Phalaropes. Whoever heard of a phalarope in Minnesota?

And it's developed into a social event for the town as well: In spring the Sons of Norway put on an evening banquet and the town of Marietta serves a breakfast and a noon lunch for birders. Other towns in the area are jumping into the competition; with hundreds of strangers coming in from all over the world, it's getting to be a big deal out there.

Marietta sits 5 miles north of U.S. Highway 212 on County Road 7, 2 miles from South Dakota; Salt Lake is 1 mile west and 3 miles south of town.

BOX ELDER BUG DAYS
Minneota

They are a polite bug, clean and handsomely marked in red and black, formal and neatly shaped, especially when compared to box elders themselves. They don't eat crops, spread disease, smear the roads, foul the waters, buzz, bite, sting, or stink. But in September you couldn't get enough zeros on this page to number them, and they all want to get in your house and spend the winter with you.

And small towns in this state like nothing better than to identify a local nuisance and celebrate it with a weekend named after it. Farming's becoming more solitary all the time; some of those folks need to have a reason to come to town and have some fun.

It began in Minneota in 1985 as Town and Country Day, the first Saturday after Labor Day; after a few years they decided to juice it up a little with some humor, and in 1990, after local writer and poet Bill Holm assigned the insect as a poetry subject for his college students and published a book of the resulting verse, it became Box Elder Bug Day. In 1991 they added another day, and in '95 made it three days. They hide a wooden box elder bug named Olaf and the finder gets a fifty-dollar bill; they have a street dance, a beer garden, a queen and her court (". . . yes, child, your grandma Britney was once the Box Elder Bug Queen of Minneota, Minnesota . . ."), arts and crafts stands, a kiddie parade, antique tractor plowing, a magic show, a chili cook-off, quilt shows, puppet shows, pony rides, a whopper feed, bull riding, a softball tournament, a sheep-to-shawl weaving demonstration, along with rock bands, a horn band, a Dixieland band, a Grand Parade, a sporting clay shoot, and a lot more—including, of course, box elder bug races.

You race your box elder bug on the same track you race your wood tick; athletes start in the center of the circle and the first to reach the outer ring wins. If they panic and fly it's a match disqualification. No exceptions: gotta have at least one of the six feet on the track at all times. You can buy racing bugs at the Bug Market there, and you can also buy a book of authentic box elder bug poems.

Box Elder Bug Days are first weekend after Labor Day in Minneota. For information call the Minneota Area Chamber of Commerce at (507) 872–6790.

G L O C K E N S P I E L
N e w   U l m

There are two tons of brass bells hanging in a 45-foot tower smack in the middle of this city. The biggest bell, a low C, weighs 595 pounds, and together with its associates it plays a series of tunes every day at noon, 3:00 P.M., and 5:00 P.M.; when the bells play, figurines in the tower dance, seemingly in spite of themselves.

This is an analog timepiece, with four clock faces with huge hands and a lot of gears and very few microchips, harking back to an age when there were only one or two clocks in a whole town and the knowledge of the correct time was held by very few. The tolling of the time sent a message of power beyond the imagination of the average miserable peasant—later to become our ancestor—and was a source of pride and wonder. Time wasn't something you carried around back then; you got it from the authorities, when they wanted to give it to you. Now children carry time on their wrists more precise than observatories in those old days. Digital timepieces sell for the price of an hour's pay at an analog hamburger joint, or free for opening a bank account.

With analog time this large you also get large analog music, real bells with real strikers inside, and you don't have the options you get with your digital devices, such as the type of ringer and the tune—for instance, you can't choose a Hungarian Dance or the Hokey-Pokey or the Waltz Militaire, or even the Regular Ring. The options belong to the person at the keyboard, and you get what they give. But it's free. It's not only free, but you get it whether you want it or not. There's a lesson in there, children; who can tell me what it is?

Thanks to donations from people in thirty-one states and fifty-one Minnesota towns, people in New Ulm always know the time—without having to wear a watch or boot-up a computer.

New Ulm, a city of 14,000, is a natural place for the first freestanding carillon clock tower in the United States. It was built here in 1980 with donations from people in thirty-one states and fifty-one Minnesota towns, and it fits right in with the town's ongoing celebration of all things Germanic. It was settled that way on purpose, by a contingent of Chicago immigrants from the province of Württemberg, where Ulm is the main city, and has kept many of the original names, costumes and holidays. Oktoberfest and Fasching are big here: lots of lederhosen and polka bands, a time of tubas, bratwurst, accordions, and beer.

Hermann the German keeps watch over New Ulm's 14,000 residents.

On a high hill overlooking the city stands the heroic figure of Hermann the German, sword upraised but with a wing missing from his helmet, apparently knocked off in a storm; they are selling Hermann bobblehead dolls to raise money for repairs. Hermann the German was the man who freed them from the rule of the Romans—this was back in Europe, of course, but it's kept the Romans from bothering them over here as well.

The Glockenspiel is in Schonlau Plaza, 4th North and Minnesota Street, in New Ulm. For information call (507) 354–4111.

BANDWAGON

*A*n obituary notice captioned CHUCK PASEK—TV HOST, 76 read as follows:

> MANKATO, Minn.—Chuck Pasek, the longtime host of a weekly television program featuring polka and old-time music, died Tuesday after a long illness. He was 76.
>
> Mr. Pasek was the host of "Bandwagon" on KEYC-TV in this southern Minnesota city for more than 30 years until he retired in 1995. Mr. Pasek also was program director for many years while working on air as sports director, then as a news anchor.
>
> Before going into television, Mr. Pasek did sports and news reporting for KYSM-AM in Mankato.

A nice little notice but not that unusual—except that it was printed in the San Diego Union-Tribune. *His wife wrote: "I received notes, letters & cards from people all over the US—old Mankato residents that had grown up listening to him. His death was carried in many cities in the US."*

The show is still carrying on, the longest-running live polka show in the country. The Mankato Free Press *ran a story on the show's amazing longevity twenty-three years ago. "The Bandwagon Show has been so successful it's almost embarrassing," wrote Tim DeMarce "In the last 10 years the show has always been in the top 10 of all Nielsen-rated programming on the station, including the best that CBS has to offer."*

Bandwagon went on the air March 30, 1961, when the station itself was only a year and a half old. It's always been local bands and local dancers, people whose friends are watching them on television. Chuck Pasek once said: "Why, they come in here on Monday nights, and they're celebrating their 50th wedding anniversary, and Mom's in a long gown, and Dad's in his best suit, and they've got boutonnieres on, and they slip me a note to say they're in the audience. Their relatives are all at home watching, and after they leave here they'll go out and buy Ma dinner. I can't hardly ignore it. That's golden. . . . We try to make 'em part of the show."

It's been forty years of fun, and a hitch or two; a streaker furnished a memorable *Bandwagon* moment back in the 1960s. And a man fell down with a heart attack on the dance floor one week and was back the next.

They do receive the occasional complaint. Pasek was quoted: "They're mostly from people who weren't raised around here, some professor from the college or somewhere. I call 'em the 'intelligencia.' They say it's corny, but I don't argue with 'em. I've never claimed it was great art." Pasek became the "sex symbol of the over-60 set," getting him squeals from the ladies and sometimes packages of dressed chickens, or pork chops, or homemade bread. He said, "They're really nice people, and if this is what they enjoy instead of Beethoven, then that's their right."

Bandwagon is recorded Monday nights at 8:00 P.M. at the KEYC-TV studios, 1570 Lookout Drive in North Mankato. Dancers are welcome. It is broadcast the following Saturday from 6:00 to 6:30 P.M. central time. For more information, call (507) 625–7905. Tell 'em we sent you.

CHARLES HANSON DUCK COLLECTION
Ortonville

Charles Hanson has been interested in waterbirds since he was a farm boy in the 1940s, admiring the fabulous plumage of ducks and geese brought home by his dad and uncles in hunting season. They lived near Artichoke Lake in western Minnesota, right in the middle of the migratory flyway, and he was witness to a rich variety of teal, Pintails, Mallards, Wood Ducks, Bluebills, Redheads, Canvasbacks, and Goldeneyes.

A fascination with preserving the birds put him into taxidermy and he got good at it, and when he had the chance to hunt farther afield he went, ultimately making seven trips to Alaska, for the Emperor Goose and other exotic coastal species. The Kodiak and St. Lawrence Islands yielded sea ducks: eiders, scoters, and the beautiful Harlequin Duck. The collection contains birds from everywhere, including the Baikal Teal from Siberia, the Chiloe Wigeon from South America, and the Capercaillie Grouse of northern Europe, the world's largest grouse at twelve pounds. Charles hunts birds on a one-of-each basis, as an entomologist hunts bugs; it's not about the meat. He might carry the same two shotgun shells in his pocket for weeks in the field.

The result of this life's work in the marshes of the world is one the most complete collections of waterfowl on the planet: more than 500 species, including even the extinct Labrador Duck. He didn't help this bird to extinction—it was already gone—but he put together a dead-accurate re-creation of it using markings and features from a Common Scoter, a Red-breasted Merganser, and a White Call Duck.

In addition to the waterfowl, he has gathered and displayed a large number of American Indian artifacts, vintage cars, and

*Charles Hanson is the kind of man who has all his ducks in a row—
or several rows.*

old John Deeres. He and his wife have traveled to Latin America, India, and Asia as volunteers, helping to build schools and hospitals, and he has reconstructed, moved, and donated the old Artichoke Lake Trading Post, built by his uncles of ax-hewn logs, to the Big Stone County Historical Society. It is in this original log building that his bird collection is on display, and it is most amazing; especially that one man, with help from no college, trust, or government, could have assembled and constructed what is very likely the most complete collection of waterfowl in the world.

You can see the Charles Hanson Collection at the Big Stone County Historical Society located at the junction of U.S. Highways 75 and 12.

SHOOTOUT

Some like to say that Northfield's famous bank holdup was the last battle of the Civil War, fought eleven years after the fact on the main street of a prospering northern small town. Jesse James of Missouri, who had fought with Quantrill's Raiders, was said to harbor a deep dislike for two of the First National Bank's stockholders, one a Union general and the other a notorious carpetbagger.

It happened in the nation's one hundredth year, the year Alexander Graham Bell invented the telephone; on September 7, 1876, ten weeks after George Custer and his troops were killed at the Little Big Horn and just a week after Wild Bill Hickock was shot in the head in Deadwood—and fifty-four days after the first major-league no-hitter was pitched, by George Bradley of the St. Louis Brown Stockings against the Hartford Dark Blues.

The James brothers, Frank and Jesse; Cole, Bob, and Jim Younger; along with Charley Pitts, Clell Miller, and Bill Chadwell, rode north to Northfield with more than vengeance on their minds; the bank was rumored to hold $200,000 on any given day, and a sleepy little Minnesota river town didn't seem likely to be a problem. After ten years of successful armed robbery in Missouri and Kentucky, they were well dressed, well armed, and well ponied. And they were cool.

Northfield was a town of hardworking farmers, millers, and storekeepers, mostly of Swedish descent, and eight strangers riding in on fine horses and wearing suits and fancy long coats and shiny black boots, Colts on the hip and new Winchesters in the scabbards—well, they kind of stood out. They'd never had a bank robbery in Northfield, but they had an idea of what one might look like, and this sort of had that look. Especially when Jesse, Bob Younger, and Charley Pitts went into the bank, with Cole Younger and Miller standing outside, while Frank, Jim Younger, and Chadwell sat their horses at the end of the street and didn't say much. A barber told a customer to wipe the shaving cream off his face and get ready to fight.

A hardware store owner from across the street, J. A. Allen, came over to the bank, walked up to Clell, and asked: "What's going on here, young man?" Miller is said to have replied, "Shut your damned mouth and git," and shoved him off the boardwalk. And just that quick the street was full of men with shotguns, revolvers, cleavers, knives; whatever was handy. Rifles magically appeared in upstairs windows.

And inside the bank a teller named Joseph Heywood refused to open the vault. Cole stuck his head in the door and said they had trouble outside, and Pitts gratuitously shot Heywood in the head on his way out. On the street they were met with a hail of gunfire; Miller and Chadwell were killed, Pitts was mortally wounded, and all three Younger brothers were hit, later to be captured at Madelia, Minnesota, and sent to prison.

The James boys got away; Jesse put a new Missouri gang together and robbed trains—his last four in 1881, the same year Louis Pasteur developed an immunization for anthrax. He was killed the next year by Bob Ford, another outlaw, for the ransom, and Frank turned himself in and was never convicted of anything.

They hold a reenactment, "The Defeat of Jesse James Days," the weekend after Labor Day. It's a lot of fun.

For information call the Northfield Chamber of Commerce at (800) 658–2548.

THE EMPRESS OF SEED ART
Owatonna

M innesota is perhaps not the Big Ten football force it would like to be, or the national college basketball power either, but when it comes to state fairs they take a backseat to nobody. The fair is huge, and getting a BEST IN SHOW ribbon in any category is not for rookies or wannabes. And in that environment, Lillian Colton would be the Tiger Woods of Crop Art.

In a legendary stretch from 1969 through 1982, Lillian won Best in Show twelve of the fourteen times she entered. She now has a booth at the fair where she shows others the intricacies of the art, but she doesn't compete anymore. One has the feeling it's out of not wanting to look greedy; not wanting to be likened to the New York Yankees.

She was a hairdresser, operating the Cinderella Clip 'n Curl Beauty Shop in Owatonna for sixty-seven years. Customers would bring her seeds of all colors and denominations, from alfalfa to zinnia: barley, canola, safflower, oats, cotton, flax, corn, buckwheat groats, sunflower, four o'clock and morning glory, hollyhock and poppy, citron and a hundred more, and she finds hundreds more than that. She has a 6- by 9-foot closet with shelves holding 500 jars of seeds. There are seed jars on her staircase.

She does portraits, of the modest and the famous, from neighbors to the governor. In 1999 she said, "I don't know how many people have said, Well you better make Jesse this year. So I made Jesse." And she does outdoorsmen and farmers, schoolkids and old folks; bobcats and ducks and loons and anything else she feels like doing. She's ninety years old now, no longer cutting hair but still doing amazing art, one seed at a time.

Some folks plant seeds, and some folks find other uses for them. Just ask Lillian Colton. She's created seed portraits of everyone from local farmers to schoolkids to Governor Jesse himself.

Lillian's seed portraits can be seen in the Horticulture Building at the Minnesota State Fair, which runs for the last ten days of summer, including Labor Day. The fairgrounds are located on Snelling Avenue and Como Avenue north of Interstate 94 in St. Paul.

W. W. MAYO HOUSE

William Worrall Mayo was born in 1819 in the village of Eccles, near Manchester, England. He studied medicine in Glasgow and London and sailed for America in 1845, working first in New York City's Bellevue Hospital and then moving on to the Indiana Medical College; he married Louise Abigail Wright in 1851. He didn't take a straight-line path to becoming a doctor: He was at various times a tailor, a census taker, a farmer, a justice of the peace, and a ferry boat operator. In 1854, while suffering one of a number of bouts of malaria he caught in Indiana (perhaps it's more like India than we think), he hitched a horse and wagon and told his wife he was going north: "I'm going to keep on driving until I get well or die." He found the weather to his liking and moved his family to St. Paul.

In 1859 he built with his own hands this beautiful little Gothic house at 118 North Main Street in Le Sueur. He set up his first medical practice in an upstairs room, 9 feet by 10 feet, and became known as the Little Doctor; he was 5 feet, 4 inches tall. In 1861 his first son, William James, was born in the house.

In 1863 he was appointed examining surgeon for the Civil War draft board of southern Minnesota, headquartered in Rochester, and the following year he moved his practice there, where his second son, Charles Horace, was born; ultimately the doctor and his sons founded the Mayo Clinic.

The house in Le Sueur was bought by Carson Nesbit Cosgrove; three generations of the family lived in the house from 1874 to 1920. C. N., known as the Little Giant, was 5 feet, 3 inches tall and the driving force and the first president of the Minnesota Valley Canning Company; his son Edward and his grandson Robert were each born in the house that Dr. Mayo built, and they both served long and well at the company C. N. built. In 1950, under Robert's leadership, it became the Jolly Green Giant.

Two of Minnesota's proudest organizations, both hatched in a modest but elegant white house made by the careful hands of a surgeon, in this quiet river town.

The Mayo House is located at 118 North Main Street in Le Sueur. It is open May, September, and October, Saturday only from 1:00 P.M. to 4:30 P.M., and June through August, Tuesday through Saturday from 10:00 A.M. to 4:30 P.M. Call (507) 665–3250 or (507) 665–6965 for more information.

PIPESTONE QUARRY
Pipestone

*At an ancient time the Great Spirit, in the form of a large
bird, stood upon the wall of rock and called all the tribes
around him, and breaking out a piece of the red stone
formed it into a pipe and smoked it, the smoke rolling over
the whole multitude. He then told his red children that this
red stone was their flesh, that they were made from it, that
they must all smoke to him through it, that they must use
it for nothing but pipes: and as it belonged alike to all the
tribes, the ground was sacred, and no weapons must be
used or brought upon it."*

An artist named George Catlin wrote this in 1836; it is a
Lakota account of the beginnings of pipestone. Other versions come from other of the Plains Indians: the Crow, the
Pawnee, and the Blackfeet. Stone pipes from 2,000 years ago
have been found in Ohio, but indications suggest that pipes
from this quarry were first carved sometime in the 1600s,
when Indians first acquired steel tools through trade.

Catlin had set out to document North American Indians in
oil on canvas; although he wasn't the first white man there, his
was the first published account of the quarries and of the pet-
roglyphs around the base of three nearby granite boulders,
called the Three Sisters. The Indians considered them the
guardians of the sacred red stone. The formal name of the
stone is Catlinite; a rare honor for a painter, to have an entire
class of rock named after him.

The general public didn't become aware of it until a poet began
his most famous narrative with: "On the mountains of the prairie
/ On the great Red Pipestone Quarry. . . ." This was in 1855,
Longfellow's *Song of Hiawatha*, an epic that is reenacted yearly
at the nearby amphitheater built specifically for the purpose.

Our first national monument wasn't signed into existence until 1937, when the Pipestone National Monument was opened to the public, with quarrying limited to Indians. The first park ranger was a great man, an Ojibwa named Standing Eagle, also known as George Bryan. His skill and artistry at carving pipes was such that Presidents Truman and Eisenhower were presented with them; a beautiful example hangs in the Smithsonian Institution in Washington. He carved the largest peace pipe in existence, the Buffalo Pipe, which hangs here at the visitor center.

His son Richard recently retired after twenty years with the National Park Service; he and his family carry on the legacy, carving pipes as they have been carved for hundreds of years. Patiently, and with great artistry.

You can visit the monument every day of the week throughout the year. The hours are 8:00 A.M. to 5:00 P.M., with extended summer hours. It is located north of the city of Pipestone on U.S. Highway 75, then west on County Road 67. Contact the Pipestone National Monument, 36 Reservation Avenue, Pipestone, MN 56164; (507) 825–5464.

MINNESOTA INVENTORS HALL OF FAME
Redwood Falls

The building that houses the Inventors Hall of Fame, just west of Redwood Falls, was for decades the Redwood County Poor Farm, a large and handsome brick building with arched window openings and stately evergreens in the yard, a scene that would fit nicely on a college campus. The kind of building that would make some poor people uncomfortable. But poor farms went out of style some time back, and it is now the

Redwood County Museum, where one room is given over to the Inventors Hall of Fame. It's kind of a hidden Hall of Fame, not considered a big enough deal to mention on the town's Web site, or even on the museum's Web site.

There aren't a lot of displays right now in the Hall of Fame, and it's open only in summer. The walls are hung with pictures of inducted inventors, but if you are looking for splashy displays of astounding inventions you have to wait until the second week in June, when the Minnesota Inventors Congress meets in the big Redwood Falls Community Center and conducts "the world's oldest Invention Convention."

There's wistful talk of someday building their own building and having a real Hall of Fame, but for now they are just One of the World's Least Famous Halls of Fame.

For information on the convention, which *is* famous and open to the public and draws huge crowds, call Sara Mattson at the Minnesota Inventors Congress: (800) INVENT–1 (that's 800–468–3681).

WORLD'S LARGEST EAR OF CORN
Rochester

In the game of the world's largest there is no uniformity of scale, no standard minimums or maximums; it's a lot like the old western frontier. No law at all and anything goes. For instance, everyone knows a Prairie Chicken is larger than an ear of corn, but the world's largest ear of corn is a whole lot bigger than the world's largest Prairie Chicken. Even the world's second largest ear of corn, also in Minnesota, is bigger than the world's largest Prairie Chicken.

The world's largest ear of corn also has the highest
moisture content.

And if any petty little fussbudget comes along and whines that this is just a water tower painted to look like an ear of corn so it's not really qualified, you say, if it's your tower: "What does it matter what's inside? Sure there's water in there. Do you know what's inside the world's largest Prairie Chicken? Or the world's largest otter? We admit there's water in there. Others aren't so forthcoming. Who knows what's inside some of these world's largest creatures? They could be full of Swiss cheese or Swiss francs, for all you know. The world's largest otter could be a piggy bank; but he'd still be the world's largest otter."

The world's largest ear of corn was completed in 1932 by the Chicago Bridge and Iron Company, for what was then the Reid-Murdoch Company and is now Libby Foods; it's 151 feet to the top of the light and 90 feet to the top of the standpipe, so the ear itself is 60 feet tall and has a capacity of 50,000 gallons. And it's designed to the proper proportions; counting the rows and kernels gives a standard ear of corn. The root is a bit deeper than standard; it's drilled down to what they call the Jordan level, which is about 310 feet below ground, and to the scale of the ear that's about a 16-foot root. In real life 16-foot roots would take a lot of the humor out of raising corn.

The New Yorker magazine ran a picture of it once. Mr. Al Whipple, who recently retired as the plant engineer after forty years, said it serves the canning factory on a seasonal basis. They start in spring with peas, moving on to lima beans, sweet corn, carrots, and mixed vegetables; the season is over in November, and they spend the winter doing heavy maintenance work. The tower looks the same whether it's working or not; its main job is to be an ear of corn anyway, and it does that year-round.

It's easily seen from the intersection of U.S. Highways 14 and 63 in south Rochester.

SULLIVAN'S JEWEL BOX

*T*he mechanical butter churn was invented in Owatonna in 1889, and by the time Louis Sullivan came to town in 1906 the place was known as the Butter Capital of the World, producing more butter in 16 square miles than any other 16 square miles anywhere in the known universe. After the opening of the Farmers' National Bank building in July 1908, they were still first in butter but they were also home to "Sullivan's Jewel Box"—the last masterpiece in the career of the man who invented the skyscraper and who is arguably our greatest and most influential architect.

If you were to visit but one architectural landmark in the state, this would be the one; in 1958 the Postal Service featured it on the eighteen-cent stamp, one of only four buildings in the United States so honored. The reason for all the hullabaloo is that it's gorgeous.

He couldn't have done it without a willing client. Carl Bennett was vice president of the Farmers' National Bank and was given the job of seeing to the completion of a new building. He had earned a degree in fine arts from Harvard in 1890 but gave up his plans for a career as a concert pianist to return to the family business. And although he was a dedicated family man and a strong Baptist, he selected a nocturnal hard-drinking agnostic architect. They built a mutual respect and a lasting friendship.

Bennett's collaboration with Sullivan and draftsman George Grant Elmslie, Chicago artist Louis Millet, and sculptor Kristian Schneider produced a building that created a sensation among critics and architects, as well as in the banking trade. The remodeling in 1958 drew the attention of the New York Times: ". . . In 1908 the design was perfect, and it was functional. A noted Dutch architect, Dr. Hendrick Berlage, considered it superior to any-

thing of its kind in Europe. In recent years architects have recognized it as one of the great buildings in the United States."

Sullivan himself fondly called it a "color symphony," probably as good a description as any of the fabulous interior. Go there.

The bank is located at the intersection of Broadway and Cedar Avenue in downtown Owatonna. Bankers' hours there are 8:00 A.M. to 5:30 P.M. Monday through Friday and Saturday 8:00 A.M. to noon. For a tour of the bank call Julie Troft at (507) 455–7500.

Built in 1908, Sullivan's Jewel Box was the last masterpiece in the career of the man who invented the skyscraper.

SOD HOUSE ON THE PRAIRIE
Sanborn

It's an unlikely teenage dream come true, this simple one-room house made of dirt. Stan McCone's great-grandparents homesteaded in South Dakota in the 1880s; he himself moved from Iowa to this western part of Minnesota in the 1970s and finally in 1987 began work building the house that had been bugging him since he was teenager, the replication of his tall-grass ancestral home.

It sits just a few miles up U.S. Highway 14—officially the Laura Ingalls Wilder Historic Highway—from Walnut Grove and the banks of Plum Creek. It's 21 by 36 feet, the walls are 2 feet thick, and it features a fir plank floor and a grass roof. It's heated by firewood, lit by oil, watered from a bucket hauled in; there's an outhouse back behind somewhere and that's made of sod, too. And if this all sounds like fun to you, you're not alone. Stan and his wife, Virginia, have turned it into a B&B and if you have a mind to stay there you need to sign up ahead of time.

Stan cut the sod from a neighbor's field, a hard-to-find patch of virgin prairie. He rode a horse-drawn sled with side blades and center cutter to slice it into strips, which he cut with a knife into 2-foot lengths. They were hauled 4 miles on a hay wagon and then stacked in double rows for the walls; he said the wall would settle as much as 18 inches during drying, for which the builders would have to make allowance when they put in the wooden window and door frames.

With its decent floor and plastered walls, Stan calls this his rich man's soddy. A hundred twenty years ago it would have cost about fifty dollars. He has also built a more typical house of the era, the poor man's soddy, smaller, with a dirt floor and

We sure don't build 'em like we used to.

leaky roof and a price tag closer to five bucks, to show visitors a more accurate version of the hard realities of the time. There were no courthouses or railroad depots, no concert halls or corporate headquarters, ever made of sod; Stan's rich man's soddy is about as good as sod construction ever got.

Virginia has furnished it with two beds, a fainting couch with a buffalo robe, gingham curtains, books on sod house living, and a set of Wilder's works, and she brings guests breakfast in the morning: turnovers, bacon, eggs, and coffee, on dishes from the time. The surrounding acreage has been restored to bluestem prairie grass and wildflowers.

Visitors come from as far away as Japan: birders, history fans, Wilder readers, ordinary curiosity seekers. Virginia says, "Everyone who stays here, no matter where they're from, goes home feeling refreshed. They get a chance to get away from television and cell phones and to realize what's important again: spending some real time with people you care about."

The Sod House is located 1 mile east and ¼ mile south of the junction of U.S. Highway 71 and US 14 near Sanborn. It's open daily April through October. Call (507) 723–5138 for information.

THE CAIRN OF PEACE
Vernon Center

At a rest area half a mile north of Vernon Center on U.S. Highway 169 stands a dignified rectangular monument built of Kasota stone. In the face are set twenty stones, each from a different country; two are newer than the rest, from Northern Ireland and Yugoslavia, both of which finally arrived thanks to a determined citizen from each of the two countries. Why they were missing in the first place is a mystery—perhaps somehow lost or misplaced during construction—but they are in place now and they complete the chronicle of a remarkable event.

Just across the road from here, on the farm of Mr. Bert Hanson, people from around the world gathered in 1972 for the first-ever Farmfest, held in conjunction with the nineteenth Annual World Ploughing Contest. "Ploughing" is similar to what we call "plowing" except it has a more international feel to it and it's done on a smaller scale; nothing like our monster ten-bottom plows and eight-wheel-drive articulated tractors.

The contestants from the twenty nations used tractors we
don't see around here: Steyr, David Brown, Leyland, and Deutz,
along with the more familiar Massey-Ferguson and Ford.
Ploughs carried names like Fiskar, Gassner, and Kverneland.
Accounts from the time don't go into the arcane details of judg-
ing the ploughing, but one gets the impression that it's a quiet
and precise activity—as opposed to, say, the tractor pull, which
is all noise and horsepower.

Speaking of which, there were quite a few politicians on hand
for that first Farmfest, held in an election year; George McGovern made a campaign speech and Nixon's secretary of agriculture, Earl Butz, made a counterspeech, and a number of others
put in appearances. Roy Rogers and Dale Evans did a show
here, and country singer Charlie Pride sang for 50,000 who
broke into applause at the beginning of every tune. Bob Hope
drew 80,000 people; a couple was sent here on a date by *The
Dating Game,* along with a chaperone. The Air Force Thunder-
birds put on an low-altitude high-speed spectacular that raised
the adrenaline level in the county to unheard-of levels.

It was quite the deal. And when it was all over, stones from
the twenty competing nations were quietly set in place in a
monument by a patient stonemason named Bud Reed—placing
temporary ones for the two that showed later—and everyone
went home. A woman who operated an overworked grocery
store in nearby Garden City said of the foreign visitors: "I'll tell
the world—those people were the most wonderful people I have
ever met."

A bartender in Vernon Center said: "They were much better
behaved than some of our people."

An elderly woman expected "sit-ins and maybe demonstrations" when McGovern spoke, but she said, "It's surprising, but
there weren't any hippies in town."

The Cairn of Peace can be seen on U.S. 169, north of Vernon
Center on the way to Mankato.

GIANT CANADIANS

*I*n the 1920s the Mayo family in Rochester had a
small flock of captive geese at their cabin southwest
of town on Mayowood Lake, on the Zumbro River.
Migrant geese from Canada dropped in out of curiosity and found out they were relatives. And according to
Minnesota custom, once they found a place at the relatives' where they could stay for free they came back the
next year, and they brought the kids with 'em, too.
They began to drop in, so to speak, on their way down
to Mardi Gras. And drop in again on the way back.

And in 1947 a grateful patient of the Mayo Clinic
who had heard about the family geese donated twelve
bigger geese from Nebraska, to be released on Silver
Lake right there in the middle of town. Well, bigness
seems to draw more bigness, and that dozen caught the
attention of a few quite larger geese; the newcomers
liked the warm water from the power plant so much
they stayed all winter, and next year there were more.
Biologists had believed the Giant Canada Goose to be
extinct, but on a fine morning in January 1962 they
came to town and were able to confirm that this alien
bunch were indeed the last known Branta canadensis
maxima. They are the largest of the eleven nations of
Canada geese, weighing eleven to fourteen pounds
apiece and sporting wingspans of nearly 6 feet. Their
next-largest relatives weigh from eight to ten pounds,
and even that seems like a lot of weight to fly with.

Now, at the peak of migration in a typical year,
downtown Rochester is home to 30,000 to 35,000 giant
geese, one big goose for every household. At 10 pounds

per bird, that would be 300,000 pounds: 150 tons of goose, three times the weight of both houses of the Minnesota legislature, and you could throw in a good-sized governor to boot. In a small park setting, 150 tons of just about any creature deposits a considerable daily slipperyness to the landscape, and a crabby minority of the citizens of Rochester would be just fine with it if everyone just grabbed their goose and they all had a big old barbecue.

But the majority are proud of the city's giant geese. The Rochester Visitor *says, "The waterfowl using Silver Lake are an integral part of the Rochester community. . . . and even though Minnesota's seasons change, the beauty and magic of Silver Lake's giant Canada geese stays the same." The ordinary person is moved once more to ask: So is this a great country or what?*

HOTEL CATS
Wabasha

The Anderson House is a comfortable residential hotel, built in 1856 of red brick with white wood trim and a modest hexagonal tower on the corner. It's real appeal, however, is the no-cost option offered to guests: You can have your room with or without a cat. They have eleven on the staff, so you have other options as well, like age, size, and color; they have shy cats, boisterous cats, cats who could use more exercise. But they are all professionals: well behaved, immunized, skilled in the art of providing a calming presence, and steadfast in their commitment to duty, which is to sleep at the foot end of the bed and to always use the litter box.

The hotel was already known for its fabulous country menu, the giant cinnamon rolls and Grandma Anderson's Chicken Noodle soup, and its practice of offering a warm brick in a quilted envelope for cold feet, when a fellow who was traveling to and from the Mayo Clinic became a regular visitor. He told the owner of his cat who slept at the foot of his bed, and she offered to lend him one of hers while he was there. He was so pleased that cats became another hotel amenity.

The hotel has twenty-four rooms, more rooms than cats. In addition to the eleven staff cats, there are two more at the owner's house available as backups, plus two kittens in training. The full-time cats spend their off-duty hours in a room like a bunkhouse or a nursery (a felinery), with a climbing tree and a viewing window through which you select your animal. The compartments are like a Pullman sleeper, three high, each with its occupant's name on it—a formality the cats ignore. These cats are used to sleeping around.

Some visit the hotel especially for the cats: grandparents whose grandchildren can't have pets, or people whose spouses

Pick a cat, any cat. At The Anderson House, guests can choose a feline companion to keep them warm at night.

are feline-allergic. Repeat guests sometimes have a favorite cat and will offer it a retirement home. Last year a cat who had become too heavy to carry around—hard to put one on a diet and not the others—was sent to a family in Florida, who did put her on a diet and who write with regular updates and photos. She's doing well down there.

The current catkeeper says, "When I take a cat up to a guest's room I feel like Santa Claus . . . people are so glad to see them."

Contact The Anderson House, 333 West Main Street, Wabasha. For more information call (800) 535–5467 or visit www.theandersonhouse.com.

HORSE THIEF DETECTIVES

*I*n June 1862 Orrin Pease of St. Mary had two fine horses stolen; he was new to the area, and his neighbors were outraged at this terrible welcome. Three men were ultimately caught and convicted of larceny, but they broke out of jail pending appeal. It was one of many such incidents, leading people to conclude that the southeastern part of the state was infested with a gang of horse thieves.

They organized the Waseca County Horse Thief Detectives on February 16, 1864; between then and 1900 only one member lost a horse to a thief. And once the story got out that the WCHTD were after them, two suspect families left town and that was the end of it.

But the association lives on, with 1,200 members around the world, some from as far away as Oman. The current president, Wayne Breck, says: "We only meet for a picnic once a year—it's a carryover from years ago—they really had an association that met monthly and went after horse thieves and all that stuff—but there's no horse thieves around now, at least I haven't heard of any. . . . Maybe 150 people come every year, and a lot of them are descendants of early settlers in the county, way back to the 1870s—

so we just have a potluck dinner and we play games with the kids and then go home. It's only an annual thing, we don't do anything in between. We sell memberships for three dollars and you get a bumper sticker and a card and a little brochure. . . . We give prizes to the members who come from farthest away, and the newly marrieds and the new babies, and the oldest married, and stuff like that.

"We always meet on the Fourth of July, at noon, west of town here at the orchard . . . everybody knows they're supposed to be there at noon with a dish to pass, and we have a nice picnic."

Asked about the hard history, he says, "We have on record, about three or four times where they caught horse thieves, back in the late 1800s. . . . but they never actually hanged anybody in Waseca County for bein' a horse thief. Mainly the organization was to alert all the farmers to look out for each other."

The membership card specifies three obligations:

- "I am obligated to keep a sharp lookout for stolen horses; to return them to their rightful owners and to aid in discouraging horse thieves.
- "At the call of the Captain of the Riders, I shall mount my best horse in pursuit of thieves and carry a rope for use by the Vigilante Committee if so ordered.
- "I will not leave my saddle during posse duties except for fatigue and/or other reasons."

Contact the Waseca County Horse Thief Detectives, Mr. Wayne T. Breck, 432 10th Street Southeast, Waseca, MN 56093.

BULLHEAD DAYS
Waterville

You don't hear much talk about bullheads in the sporting world; you never see them on the covers of *Sports Afield* or *Outdoor Life* or *Fishing World*. They don't have scales and they don't get big like their catfish relatives; they have floppy whiskers and are shaped in the classic Don Rickles physique: wider across the mouth than the chest. Not to put too fine a point on it, but they're an ugly nuisance. When the bullhead herd gets large, they muddy up the water and make it unusable for both game fish and waterfowl, they have sharp spines that sting when swimmers step on them, and they pretty much seem bent on destroying every lake in the state. All of which means that bullheads, like a lot of other bottom feeders, have a real public relations problem.

Problems have a way of finding each other, and when Waterville needed something to build a spring festival around they turned to the nasty bullhead population in Lake Sakatah. Early in June members of the sportsman's club go into the lake with nets and haul out anywhere from 8,000 to 16,000 bullheads, skin 'em with pliers, clean 'em, cut off the heads, and lower them into boiling oil; one of those things that sound bad in print but in fact are a lot of fun.

Besides the big fish feed, Bullhead Days have featured events like tractor pulls, demolition derbies, water parades, pickup pulls, horse rides, and fireworks on Sakatah Bay. Refreshing beverages are made available and they crown a queen, tactfully titled Miss Waterville. We talked to a contestant from twenty-plus years ago, Julie Gross. She said she was sixteen at the time and didn't have any talent other than her cheerleader pom-pom routine. The lady who ran it said, "Well if you don't have no talent, why don't you clean a pail of bullheads?" Julie said she knew how to fish but had to learn how to skin bullheads.

They had the usual formal part, and they modeled sportswear instead of the usual bathing suits, and then came the talent contest. She wore bib overalls, a straw hat, and her dad's old boots. She had a pail of about twenty bullheads and asked the woman how many she should do; the woman said she better do 'em all.

She told a couple of stories as she cleaned, sitting there behind three pails: a regular pail, where "they were floppin' around alive," a second pail for the good part of the bullhead, "and then the guts and the skins went in the other pail."

"It's something that you'll never forget. . . . and you know how the older ladies like to get the front seats? It was in the school cafeteria where we had it, and I was up on a platform. The guts were flyin' in the pail and all around, and all I could see were these little old ladies covering their faces. . . . I ended up gettin' first runner-up. The girl who sewed her own clothes was second attendant and the girl who sang was crowned Miss Waterville."

Word has it that if you go to the festival you should get there early and get your basket of deep-fried fillets and your bread, because it's usually sold out before Saturday night.

Bullhead Days are held the first full weekend of June, Thursday through Sunday. Call the chamber of commerce at (507) 362–4609 for more information.

MARRIAGE MILL

*T*he republic was founded with a few specific duties given to the federal government, like raising an army, but most of the lawmaking given to the various states. The founders knew about regional differences and left the hammering-out process to the locals. Combining this wonderful tolerance with a sensible economic system meant a lot of state borders offered business opportunities; this is why Minnesota is today bracketed east and west by fireworks and Sunday liquor.

Forty years ago the southern border of the state drew young people from Iowa, and especially from the Waterloo area, who wanted to get married and didn't feel like waiting. Word had it that up around Preston you could get a waiver of the three-day waiting period, and for a few years some people in town were doing a modest business in out-of-state late-night quickie marriages.

They don't like to talk about this in the current climate of obsessive responsibility, but it may not have been as bad as it sounds. Much as politicians like to stand up and shovel out ever more restrictive laws, especially as regards the behavior of reckless youth, some of us consider the idea of kids getting liquored up and running off and getting married to be preferable to them getting liquored up, running off, and not getting married.

There's no monument there to these few years of history, of course, but it would be interesting to know how many of those who sneaked across and were married without the wait—and it wasn't illegal—are still married; and how many children are walking around as grown-ups who would not exist at all if not for that judge signing that stack of waivers for the clerk of court and the two justices of the peace. Who all, by the way, got in hot water over it; the lid came off when a couple had a car accident on their way home and were questioned by troopers.

But one has to wonder: Did any of those couples, or any of their children, ever come back and thank those guys?

S T A N D S T I L L   P A R A D E
W h a l a n

A thin line, it is, between wackiness and brilliance: Ptolemy's notion that the world was round is a case in point, and so is Dave Harrenstein's idea that if a town is so small that a parade can't move in it, then the parade should stand still and the crowd should move. It gets back to physics: In the case of the parade, you have an organized rectangular solid (sort of) confined to a rectangular space and you have a disorganized fluid, the spectators, able to flow around it, and what could be more sensible?

Whalan is a town of 94, 84, 68, or 64 people, depending on your source, sitting along the abandoned Milwaukee Road tracks; the rail line is now the beautiful Root River Bicycle Trail and site of the wildly popular Sykkle Tur (Norse, of course, for "bicycle tour"). Towns along the trail hold festivities to open the season in the middle of May; in 1996 Fountain put on a sausage and pancake breakfast, Rushford had historic tours, Peterson opened a museum, and Lanesboro had an all-city garage sale. Preston held a trout-fishing contest for kids and grown-ups. And Whalan had a Standstill Parade that ended up on the CBS Television news.

In the five parades since, and all the festivities on the side, they've had bluegrass bands, square dancing, kids' tractor pulls, bed races, antique cars, a display of American flags, rummage sales, book sales, and boxing demonstrations. Floats of all kinds and constant lefse, made right there and best when it's warm. And live snakes and lizards, live exotic birds, a Norwegian display; face painting, plate painting, soap making, lace making, quilting, and crocheting. Pony rides, petting zoos, a calliope, nonmarching bands, and free blood-pressure checks.

An organic farmer dumped a wheelbarrow of dirt on the street and planted green things, and a masseuse gave free massages. A man from Rushford sat in his mint 1932 Packard Super 8 and a fellow from Fountain City, Wisconsin, rode his 1884 high-wheel bicycle—a bike he once rode coast to coast. A couple showed their pet goose, dressed in a colorful outfit, and every ten minutes they'd change the outfit. And in 2000 they held a real wedding in the parade.

And the first Grand Marshal, Adeline Larson, born in Whalan in 1908, sat in a convertible and waved to people. She said, "Seems to me eighty-eight years is a long time to wait for something like that parade. I'm really too old for something like that, but, well, it wasn't so bad."

The Standstill Parade takes place in downtown Whalan on the weekend closest to Sykkle Tur, which is May 17. Whalan is east of Lanesboro on Minnesota Highway 16. Call (507) 467–2111 for information.

GREAT GOBBLER GALLOP
Worthington

Worthington's annual King Turkey Day goes back to 1939, when a flock of turkeys led, or were driven by, a parade down the main street of town; the publicity releases on the event don't mention that they went on to the processing plant while the rest of the parade took a right turn. The media were there and so were the politicians and it was a big success. Next year it was bigger yet, featured in *Life* magazine and in movie newsreels across the country.

In Cuero, Texas, a similar event had been held since 1912, sometimes with as many as 20,000 birds; it was inevitable that

a challenge would be issued—turkeys being what they are—
and in 1973 a group of handlers brought a turkey up from
Cuero to race against Paycheck, so named because he went so
fast. The Texas bird was named Ruby Begonia because she
could handle a paycheck, and she did, that year. The names are
always the same, regardless of the birds. That's because we
know turkeys, and we know they don't know the difference.
Turkeys know the difference about almost nothing, truth be
told. Change your clothes and you're a stranger to your own
birds.

The race is staged in two heats, the first up here in September and the second down there in October, at the Cuero
Turkeyfest, formerly called the Turkey Trot. (Is *Turkeyfest*
more politically correct than *Turkey Trot*?). The athletes are
chosen from wild flocks in the two counties, but the visiting
team has the disadvantage of bringing just one bird, a bird
who gets very cold in the cargo bay of an aircraft, although
they say last year it was up with the passengers. The home
bird is drafted that morning from a flock and is presumably
well rested and aggressive. In the race there is a thirty-second
penalty if the turkey flies off into the crowd or refuses to run,
and a two-minute penalty if the handler picks the bird up and
runs with it. The winner is the one with the lowest combined
time from both heats.

The winner's trophy is 3 feet tall, of walnut and gold, called
the Traveling Turkey Trophy of Tumultuous Triumph. The winner also claims the title World's Fastest Turkey. Worthington
leads the series, 15 to 11; loser gets the Circulating Cup of Con-
summate Commiseration.

Before the gobbler race on Worthington's King Turkey Day
there is a free pancake breakfast and a parade, a 5K walk for
humans, and a 10K race for humans. The Texas celebration features food as well, but of course instead of grim running they
have live music and street dances.

King Turkey Day is the second Saturday after Labor Day.
Check with the Worthington Chamber of Commerce at (507)
372–2919 for more information.

STEPHEN TAYLOR'S GRAVE

*Stephen Taylor was born in New York State on March 23, 1757;
he was with Ethan Allen's Green Mountain Boys on May 10,
1775, when on a narrow strip of land between Lake George and
Lake Champlain, in New York, they forced the British surrender of
Fort Ticonderoga. It was a surprise attack and our critical first
victory in the War of Independence from the British.*

*History records Ethan Allen as having demanded the surrender
of Fort Ticonderoga "in the name of the Great Jehovah and the Continental Congress." But there was no Continental Congress at the
time, and Virtual Vermont says "according to historian and folk-
lorist B. A. Botkin, one Israel Harris was present at the time, and
later told his grandson (the late Professor James D. Butler of Madison, Wisconsin) that Allen's actual words were 'Come out of there,
you goddam old rat!'" However delicately Ethan phrased the
demand, they did come out, surrendering without firing a shot.*

*Stephen Taylor was listed as a resident of Sheffield in Berkshire
County, Massachusetts, when six years later he went from "the 83"
and enlisted in the First Massachusetts Regiment, "for three years or
the duration." He served as an enlisted man in three different regi-
ments of General Washington's Continental army, taking a British
rifle ball in the battle of Yorktown that left him partially blind. He
was honorably discharged as a private on December 27, 1783.*

*He returned to Sheffield and then to Seneca, New York, where
he raised four children and a stepson with his wife, Abigail, who
became bedridden and died at the age of thirty-six. He applied for a
veteran's pension in 1821, stating his occupation as a farmer and
listing his assets as "5 old chairs + 1 old table, an old desk, an old
looking glass, 2 pr. old curtains, pots and pans, 4 old pails, 4 old
barrels, dishes, a churn, an ax, an old chest, 4 old books, a cow, 2
pigs, 3 fowl and a teakettle"; altogether it was worth exactly $51.89.
They granted a monthly pension of eight dollars.*

*He moved to Minnesota Territory with eleven other Taylors in
1854, at the age of ninety-seven. The locals remembered him as a
large and robust man, temperate, never known to be sick. He qualified for 160 acres of land; the grant was approved March 10, 1856.
He died in June of the following year and was buried at Money
Creek Cemetery, a landed private at the age of one hundred.*

The family moved away and his grave remained unmarked until Memorial Day in 1880, when the caretaker of the cemetery, Captain Matthew Marvin, with his own money erected a stone with a brief biography. In 1933, with the assistance of the Wenonah Chapter of the Daughters of the American Revolution, the remains were moved to a memorial in Woodlawn Cemetery in Winona. The memorial is a 10- by 25-foot stone replica of Fort Ticonderoga, four high walls with towers at the four corners. A marker with a metal plate is set over the grave, inscribed:

A COURAGEOUS SOLDIER, MEMBER OF ETHAN ALLEN'S IMMORTAL BAND OF 83, WHO TOOK PART IN THE SURPRISE ATTACK ON THE BRITISH GARRISON AT TICONDEROGA AND THE ONLY REVOLUTIONARY WAR SOLDIER KNOWN TO BE BURIED IN THE STATE OF MINNESOTA.

Woodlawn Cemetery is located on the southwest side of Winona. To get there take U.S. Highway 61 south to Huff Street, turn right, and take another immediate right onto Lake Boulevard. The cemetery is a quarter mile down on your left.

Stephen Taylor was with Ethan Allen's Green Mountain Boys when they forced the British surrender of Fort Ticonderoga in 1775—the first victory in the War of Independence. One-hundred-and-fifty-six years later, a 10- by 25-foot stone replica of Fort Ticonderoga was built in his honor.

E d ' s   M u s e u m
W y k o f f

A tin of salmon from the 1950s recently exploded in Ed's Museum and coated the place with a remarkable odor; they've cleaned it up, but there are others sitting there swollen that could go any minute. They are considering drilling small holes in the bottoms to relieve the pressure, but it would take away a lot of the dramatic tension in the place. Right now it's not unlike visiting a museum of unexploded hand grenades. You find yourself in a heightened state of awareness there, ready to hit the deck at any sudden noise.

The building was built in 1876, the same year the town was founded; it was a brewery and a saloon, with a harness shop in the basement. In 1915 it became a grocery store, and Ed Krueger bought it in 1933, selling the Jack Sprat line of goods. There were five grocery stores in town at the time and he did the best of any of them, but his wife passed away in 1940 and keeping things in order became difficult. In the late 1960s and '70s, Ed kept the place open but also took work as a painter, specializing in church steeples; he'd go to work early and then come back and open the store and sell pop and candy bars for the kids. The counter remains the way he left it, the slumbering candy bars still there along with the unstable canned goods.

Mainly what Ed left behind was a huge and complicated mess, but he deeded it all to the city in his will, stipulating that it be made into a museum. After his passing in 1989 local women took on the project and turned it into a detailed odyssey of a man's life through most of the twentieth century, as recorded in a small-town grocery store. It's an amazing place, containing everything Ed ever owned, right down to his gallstones. In another little jar are his gold teeth. They also have his last cat, Sammy, in a plastic shroud in a cardboard box sitting on a shelf in the basement.

Esther Evers with Ed's last cat, Sammy.

They have three sets of Jack Sprat figurines in the original boxes, very valuable, and the Shirley Temple dishes that used to come in cereal boxes. Ed had a son named Fred and all his toys—even though they were well used and shared—went back into the original boxes.

To get to Ed's from I–90, take Minnesota Highway 16 at Dexter, go 22 miles to Minnesota Highway 80, and take a left into Wykoff. Ask at the Bank Gift Haus for a tour or call (507) 352–4205.

FALLS FLYER

*I*n April 1941 the U.S. Patent Office issued patent number
126,583 to Paul G. Larson of Little Falls, Minnesota, titled
"Design for a Boat" and described therein as ". . . a new, original and ornamental Design for Boats. . . ," which was an
understatement. As the first boat ever granted a U.S. patent,
Larson's Falls Flyer could have been called "a stunning, dramatic departure from the ordinary, whose speed and grace
will bring astonishment and envy to all who see it."

Paul Mikkelson owns a classic and antique boat museum
in Willmar, of which his family's 1956 Falls Flyer, bought
new, is a central attraction. "In their time, they were just
blistering. Fastest boat on the lake. No one could hold a can-
dle to it," he said. "I learned to water-ski behind it, and I
dated my wife in it. It's the same boat, the same engine.
Nothing's changed." Only 200 were ever made, all from 1939
to 1960, and the Mikkelson Collection has 17 of them. Of
these, they have the only single-cockpit inboard Speedster
version produced, both of the two split-cockpit inboard versions known to exist, and one of only two 21-foot Deluxe
Inboards ever built.

Early versions of the Falls Flyers—named after Little
Falls and its famous son, Charles Lindbergh—were of canvas stretched tight over oak frames and smooth cedar strips.

Later models were of fiberglass, but they were all of the same rounded streamlined style, closer to a race car than an open boat; sleek as fish.

Beautiful as they are, there is more to the museum than the Falls Flyers; there are a hundred vintage outboard motors on stands, all in working order. Beyond the Johnsons, Mercurys, and Evinrudes, one finds brands like Scott-Atwater, Champion, Neptune, Clark, Wisconsin, Martin, Bendix, Lockwood-Ash, Koban, Waterman, Caille, and Elto. There is also a collection of manually operated outboards, both hand and foot models, and 500 elderly toy boats, of all styles and materials and sizes. There is a great collection there of toy outboard motors: wind-ups, electric, steam-powered, gas-powered, plus the child's most trusted power of all: rubber band.

The Flyers steal the show, naturally, as they have since the first one was built in 1939, and as they still do, on any lake they cruise. They have the presence of a vintage Ferrari, and even if they are no longer the fastest, they'll always be the sleekest and the coolest.

Contact the Mikkelson Collection Classic Boat Museum, 418 Benson Avenue Southeast, Willmar, MN 56201; (320) 231–0384.

Northwest Angle
State Forest

Angle
Inlet

75
11
11
89
72
Argyle
Warren
1
219
89
75
2
Fosston
71
Bemidji
2
Bena
Walker
Akeley
Longville
Dorset
Hackensack
64
Moorhead
34
Pequot
Lakes
94
Pine River
Rothsay
Cuyuna
New York
Mills
Crosby
Fergus Falls
Motley
210
Brainerd
75
71
59
Alexandria
10
Herman
27
Kensington
10
28
Starbuck
Sauk Rapids
55
94
95
Cold
St.
Princeton
Spring
Cloud

NORTHWEST

NORTHWEST

THE $110 BRIDGE
Argyle

The best thing about this bridge is not that it cost about one ten-thousandth the price of an average bridge; the best thing about it is what a sweet little bridge it is, and how good it looks sitting there.

The Red River Valley of the North is about as flat and as fertile a place as exists anywhere on the planet; topsoil there runs pure black and 5 feet deep in places. But it's known more for what it doesn't have, like surf, mountains, forests, waterfalls, tropical fish, volcanoes, painted canyons, fabulous big-city nightlife, or any of the other standard tourist attractions. Two highways and a river run through it, but there isn't a vast category of fiction written about it; it's not exactly the antebellum South.

So it's never been a hotbed of tourism, but they've made some game attempts; one of the highways through it is U.S. Highway 75, long called the King of Trails and now, in the southern part of the state, designated the Laura Ingalls Wilder Historic Highway. Back in 1920 they marked it with a 16-inch bright yellow band around the telephone poles with black block letters, a K above a T, and it was "the best-marked road in the United States." They planned for it to run from Winnipeg to Mexico City. It made it to Winnipeg and south through Sioux

City, Omaha, Topeka, and Tulsa, and then seemed to lose its identity in Texas, somewhere around Dallas; a familiar story.

But for now it's enough that it takes you through these flat and subtle fields, and past the little park at Argyle. The Lorangers' 1878 log cabin sits there, and a three-acre piece of land across the Middle River was added in 1974. They priced pedestrian bridges and then found this old well-traveled wood-slatted cattle car, moved it in, opened up the ends, and what a bargain; and that mountain goat in the Great Northern logo somehow looks right at home.

The bridge is located at the Argyle Roadside Park on U.S. 75, at the north end of town.

Big Fish Supper Club
Bena

I
t is the world's largest muskie, at 65 feet long and 15 feet wide, and it has a huge wide-open mouth; Charles Kuralt called it his favorite building in the United States. It was originally built as the Big Muskie Drive In; one of the builders was fifteen-year-old Butch Dahl, who now owns the wonderful red, white, and blue pagoda and service station three miles east, an attraction in itself. The fish is big enough that you can stand inside the mouth and have your photograph taken, an idea that seems to occur to a major portion of the passing public. All day long and every day, they lie in it as if about to be devoured, put a ladder up to it and ride it, tie a fishing line from it to their rod and reel; some back the car up to it as if they are all about to become lunch.

The big fiberglass teeth are removed in winter for safekeeping. There was at one time a hamburger stand inside the fish

*Charles Kuralt called the world's largest muskie his
favorite building in the United States.*

but that function has been incorporated into the adjacent Big
Fish Supper Club, which is shaped like a building. There is a
picture of the fish in the opening credits of *National Lampoon's
Vacation Movie,* making it a Certified World Famous Landmark, or CWFL, as if it wasn't one already.

Bena sits 32 miles east of Bemidji on U.S. Highway 2. Call
the Big Fish Supper Club at (218) 665–2333.

PAUL BUNYAN

There are Paul Bunyans in Canada and in nearly every state in the Union, except perhaps Hawaii; here in Minnesota we have the birthplace, the girlfriend, the ax, the ox, the anchor, the cradle and the grave, and five big statues of himself, including the tallest in the world. Other places may claim to have his cap or his gloves or his rattle or his pacifier or his baby shoes; it's a free country and they can claim anything they want. Nobody's going to hassle anybody over the truth here. But we also have his rifle, razor, and CB radio; his tools, phone, coins, harmonica, Zippo lighter, shovel, moccasins, his footprint, and his mailbox. There are places in Minnesota where there are no Paul Bunyan icons whatever, but in the northern part of the state odds are good that there's one down the road.

Akeley lays a rightful claim to being the birthplace, the cradle, and the world's largest P. B. statue. The stories were first published here by the Red River Lumber Company in 1914, about the time big lumbering was winding down. The statue kneels down and holds a hand out for people to sit in and have their picture taken; if he were standing he'd be 33 feet tall. They hold Paul Bunyan Days here at the end of every June; among other things, it fills Yodelin' Swede's Bar for a few days. Bemidji claims the original Paul Bunyan because they built the first statue, back in 1937. They sent a statue of Babe the Blue Ox on a national tour that year and got attention from the New York Times (something Minnesotans seem to crave) and Life magazine.

Brainerd jumped the claim in 1949 with a talking Paul Bunyan, who scares little kids by calling them by name and who holds forth in Paul Bunyan Land, where many of the icons are kept. They maintain theirs is the "most photographed statue in the world," another hard-to-disprove unlikely statement. A man in Hackensack built a huge statue of Paul's girlfriend in 1952 and gave her the melodious name of Lucette Diana Kensack, causing distress in Brainerd because they already had a Pauline they'd use in

Paul Bunyan. What a guy. Pro scouts would be salivating if he was still around.

Hackensack's Lucette Diana Kensack. One hopes that Paul knew how lucky he was to find a good-natured woman this size.

Babe the Blue Ox. Bigger than a tractor, and harder to hitch up.

parades. Lucette, unconcerned, smiles all the time, and especially when she presides over the annual Sweetheart Days and the musical Ballad of Lucette, performed by the Hackensack Light Opera Company.

Ortonville, farther south, has a huge piece of rectangular stone held up off the ground billed as Paul's anchor; Kelliher has the grave, Isle has statues of Paul and Babe, and Chisholm has a Paul in the Museum of Mining. There are twenty-six statues of or pertaining to Paul Bunyan in this state and only one gopher, making a person wonder if Paul and Babe the Blue Ox shouldn't have been the university mascot. The Minnesota Bunyans has a nice ring to it, and the Minnesota Blue Oxen isn't bad either. Or just the Lumberjacks, if foot sores and slow dumb animals don't do it—but everyone's used to the rodent, so we're stuck with it. But it's not a gopher you see on the state map; it's a photo of that huge square-shouldered stiff-looking guy and that big wide-horned blue ox. People in Minnesota don't really like gophers. They like Paul Bunyan.

GRASSHOPPER CHAPEL
Cold Spring

Minnesota is regularly beset with what we like to call "natural disasters," generally related to the weather but not exclusively; natural as opposed to "unnatural disasters," which would cover train wrecks, arson, murder, and anything else brought on by our fellow humans through carelessness, inattention, or just plain wrong thinking.

In the springs of 1856, 1865, 1873, 1874, and 1876, the area around Cold Spring was chewed up by Rocky Mountain locusts, called choppers to differentiate them from your standard-model grasshopper. These guys were 3 inches long and had eyes round as shingle nails and heads the size of the last joint of your little finger. Mostly, though, they had big jaws and they ate everything. First the young green wheat and then everything else, including pastures, gardens, the laundry off the clotheslines. They ate big holes in the hides of cattle, so that the animals had to be destroyed.

In the spring of 1877, farmers figured the months of thirty-below cold of the previous winter would have frozen whatever choppers might have been hiding around; it looked like it was going to be a good year, and it was, right up until the sunny April morning when the sky darkened and the choppers came back, this time much worse than ever before. Farmers were already far in debt and had fought back with oil fires, tar-covered sheets of metal dragged over fields, huge bulky nets; the Stearns County Board had offered bounties for choppers by the bushel, but nothing had dented the huge clouds of insects.

It was about the end of the line for most farmers, locusts for four out of five years. They were a solid Catholic community and turned to prayer, and with the help of a $10,000 donation from Governor John E. Pillsbury's own wallet they built the 16-

A chapel dedicated to the departure of thousands of unwanted guests.

by 26-foot wood-framed Locust Chapel, in Gothic Revival style, on a hill overlooking the town, as an offering in honor of the Assumption of the Blessed Virgin. A local farmer carved a wooden statue of the Mother and Child for the altar. And about four months later, on August 15, the choppers packed up and flew off and haven't been seen since.

In 1894 the building was hit by a tornado and reduced to fragments. The statue was salvaged and stored, and in 1952 they rebuilt the chapel, this time of granite. It's officially the Assumption Chapel but is more commonly known as Grasshopper Chapel, and every August 15 the bishop of St. Cloud conducts a Mass there. Over the entrance is a plaque depicting the Virgin ascending into heaven on a cloud, with two grasshoppers below.

To get to the chapel take Minnesota Highway 23 out of Cold
Spring toward St. Cloud to Chapel Street; take a right onto Pil-
grimage Road, then a left. The chapel is at the top of the hill.

NORDIC INN
Crosby

Well, here's something different: A Minnesotan gets a wacky
idea and works at it like a madman and his neighbors
think he's crazy and after a while it all seems to turn out okay.
In this case it's a man who left northern Minnesota, joined the
navy, got out, and ended up with a pretty decent job in a California biotech company; got sick of that and moved back to his
hometown and opened a medieval B&B in an old Methodist
church.

He was given the name Richard Edward Schmidthuber and
it worked all right for him up until he became the builder of an
ancient Viking castle. Now he goes by Steinarr Elmerson, has a
full beard and long curly hair, and dresses in the kind of out-
fits that allow a person to walk around in public carrying a
battle-ax without anyone becoming alarmed; the ax fits right
in. (They might still give him a problem at the airline security
gate, but no more than anyone else: Ax, nail clipper, it's all the
same these days.)

You'd think they'd welcome new enterprise up there where
the farms are shutting down and the mines are already closed,
but it was like pulling teeth for him to get a license, even as a
homeboy. All part of the Viking struggle, apparently; first
crossing the North Atlantic in open single-mast rowboats, and,
generations later, four months of public hearings trying to get
a liquor license in Minnesota.

The Nordic Inn is the only place in Minnesota
where people over the age of two are encouraged
to eat with their fingers.

When you stay there you get the full treatment: soap cut
from a big block with a hatchet (your choice of birch or cedar),
a wake-up call from a big long curved horn, deer antlers for
toilet paper holders. You dine in a marauder's outfit and eat
with your fingers and a blunt knife, and you become part of an
interactive mystery theater with local actors.

There are five rooms at the inn: the Look Out up on top in
the steeple; Odin's Loft, with the bed in a longboat projecting
over the Great Hall; the Jarl's Den and Freya's Boudoir, both
done in appropriately medieval Scandinavian decor; and, down
below, the Vikings Locker Room, with pennants on the walls,
Astroturf carpet, yard markers, goalposts at the headboards,
and a double-nozzle shower.

And if you happen to stop by on game day you might well miss the host; he's also informal mascot for the Minnesota Vikings football team. Been on television, too.

The Nordic Inn Medieval Brew & Bed is at 210 1st Avenue Northwest, Crosby 56441. Call (218) 546–8299 for information.

WOOD TICK RACING
Cuyuna

Wood tick racing is all match racing. Two sprinters are placed in the center of a 33-inch-diameter circle, on the bull's-eye; the crowd presses in, wagers are waged, and the arthropods are released under the expert eyes of seasoned judges—some seasoned to the point of pickled—and whichever arrives first at the outer circle lives to race again. The loser, having no clue as to what was at stake in his little trip across the plywood, is smashed flat, giving real meaning to the term *single elimination.* And at the end of the long day of matches, the final lone standing Supreme Champion Racing Wood Tick is celebrated with raised mugs and loud huzzahs, bets are paid off, and then, at his crowning triumphant tick moment, he's smashed flat, too.

Persons who live in city apartments and never walk the Minnesota woods might wince at this, but most of us who have hosted a wood tick for any length of time—behind the knee, say, or in the hair—generally find it most gratifying. No reading of the Miranda rights even, much less the appointment of an attorney; it's just lights-out, you little bloodsucker: We know your intentions. You were lucky to make it this far.

The first wood tick races were held here in 1979, three guys sitting in the Cuyuna Bar after working on a pasture fence line, having a beer and picking the wood ticks off, putting

Gentlemen start your engines. Professional racing at its highest level.

them in an ashtray; they make a break for it and the bar's owner, Bill Simons, bets on which one will make it to the edge of the bar first. Inspiration hits, they make a circle on a piece of cardboard, and a new sport begins. The next year it goes public, including printed rules and a plywood field. No spurs, no supercharged ticks, and so forth. In 1982 the crowds get bigger, augmented by bikers, and in 1985 the Cuyuna Bar changes hands after the passing of Bill Simons and becomes the Woodtick Inn, creating a natural pun. (How far is the Woodtick Inn?) The race has grown every year, drawn the attention of the media, and is keeping the last remaining retail operation afloat in a town of 165; it's a tick-based economy, sort of like the watch industry in Switzerland.

On June 8, 2002, they staged the twenty-third Running of the Ticks in Cuyuna, drawing close to a thousand visitors. The town was named after the miner who founded it, Cuyler Adams, who took the first half of his name and added to it his dog's name, Una. Appropriate for a town now famous for ticks to be named after a prospector and a dog.

To get to the Woodtick Inn, take Minnesota Highway 210 to Crosby, then go north on County Road 31 for about 3 miles to Cuyuna. For information call (218) 546–5313.

You don't know the players if you don't have a scoreboard.

BACHELORMANIA

In 1992 a survey of twenty young women in Herman found that not one of them planned to stay in town after high school graduation, and just before that a young couple had moved away simply because the wife couldn't find a job. They had an eligibility ratio of 6 to 1—78 bachelors and 12 single women, out of a total of 458 citizens. The odds were bad for the men and they weren't getting better, and then in 1994 they surprised even themselves and actually did something about it.

What they did was so shocking it drew national attention: They just came right out and asked. They went public in February, said they wanted women to come to the Grant County Fair in July for a big Bachelormania. Television, radio, newspaper people picked up on it. The town's economic development coordinator, a farmer named Dan Ellison, appeared on the Today *show. The word was that they wanted women to come to town not only to meet the bachelors but also to stay and start businesses, and by May Dan was so busy with all the publicity he had to hire help for the crops.*

They drew something like 20,000 to the event; the Prairie Cafe was selling T-shirts that read BACHELORTOWN, USA. YOU CATCH 'EM, WE FEED 'EM. *Bachelors from outlying towns drove in, and hundreds of women arrived from California, Florida, Oklahoma; all over the country. And for every Herman bachelor there was a camera crew and a microphone; one showed his driver's license to verify he was for real, and said he'd met about twenty women. "Most of 'em are pretty nice people. I would say I'm kinda inexperienced. Single women don't seem to like me for some reason. I'm not quite their type."*

There were singles dances and bachelor bingo—twenty-five women playing bingo for a date with one of five men—all four nights of the fair. By Friday and Saturday things were moving along fairly well, to the point that the manager of the only bar in town, a woman named Sally, was using a police escort to take the bar's money to the nearby bank.

Nobody just up and got married on the spot, but a few couples met and corresponded. The organizers made plans to repeat it in 1995. Dan Ellison himself proposed in December 1995 and the lady accepted; the national media haven't reported if they are yet married. And a few new businesses were started in the town. The population jumped by sixty.

A movie was made about the event, Herman USA, although it wasn't filmed in Herman—it was cheaper closer to the Twin Cities, so they shot it in New Germany. And they released it nationally on September 20, 2001, at a time when nobody was in the mood to go to movies.

So Bachelormania faded, replaced by an annual Iron Pour wherein they heat scrap iron to 2,700 degrees and pour it into sand molds to make sculpture, and they have a parade and a liars' contest. It draws enough artists from out of town that some people lock their doors, so you know it's probably a pretty good time. A good place to meet people.

R ESTAURANT C APITAL OF THE W ORLD
D o r s e t

D orset lays claim to this title with the low resident-to-restaurant ratio of 5.5 to 1: They have four restaurants and twenty-two people. And it's not on a main road from one big place to another; it's up there in lake country between Nevis and Park Rapids, about a block long at the intersection of the Heartland Bicycle Trail and the two-lane "Interstate 226."

They have a few other stores—antiques, books, gifts, and bike rental—and a newspaper, the *Dorset Daily Bugle,* published once a year. It is a paper with such great respect for accuracy as to apply it very sparingly, even on its masthead. They inform us of such events as the upcoming Running of the Skunks: 11,000 men will run through the winding streets with 2,000 skunks, a century-old event expected to draw 100,000 spectators. They are also anticipating a crowd of 55,000 at the X-treme Full-Contact Tag-Team Indoor Fishing Championship event, held in the big Dorset Bowl, which has been flooded up to the thirty-fourth row for year-round fishing ever since Dorset sold off both its pro football and pro baseball teams.

They report that a local biotech firm has developed a method of extracting blood from mosquitoes using a powerful vacuum chamber and is presently working on a giant hammer to recover blood from wood ticks; both processes would help reduce the shortage of emergency supplies. A local critic claims the investors are the ones being sucked dry, which the company rejects. Another story details the opening of the new Dorset Antique Rocks store; many of the rocks are said to be thousands of years old and are in "mint condition," according to the owner.

The restaurants have been reviewed by outside observers; a typical arugula-crazed Minneapolis food critic gave them passing marks, which is exactly what you want. Rave reviews from high-tone critics generally mean the food tastes weird and you don't get much of it, plus the service is slow. The restaurants are, from north to south on the boardwalks: the Dorset General Store & LaPasta Italian Eatery (family dining, Italian, wine, beer); the Dorset Cafe (chicken, steak, ribs, seafood, drinks); Compañeros (Mexican food, drinks); and the Dorset House (family dining, evening buffet, soda fountain, beer and wine).

The reader is cautioned that with neither post office nor city government the precise population figure is subject to interpretation; locals say it "depends on who's around at the time."

Take Minnesota Highway 34 for 6 miles east of Park Rapids or 6 miles west of Nevis, to Interstate 226; go north about a mile.Visit their Web site at www.dorsetmn.com.

KENSINGTON RUNESTONE
Kensington and Alexandria

If it was a practical joke it backfired and caused more trouble than humor, but if it was a hoax it was a darn good one; and if it's the real thing like the supporters say it is, well, then it should be in the history books. It's a debate not likely to be settled soon, given the weight of experts on both sides. But at the museum in Alexandria, of course, the word *hoax* is like the invisible two-ton elephant in the room.

Still, without the suspicion there'd be no runestone industry. If everyone had said, "Okay, well, it looks good to me, and if you say so I guess there probably was a Norwegian in Minnesota 130 years before there was an Italian on the East Coast; okay, fine," the whole thing would have disappeared among the boring historical facts we all forget about. But because of the skepticism, some 12,000 people a year visit the Runestone

The cornerstone of the great controversy.

Museum in Alexandria, and who visits where Columbus first
set foot? Who even knows what state it's in? If you can prove it
for sure—whatever it is—it's going to lose appeal; it's the third
rule of show business. (The first one is well known, and the
second one says, "Yes, there is one every minute, and every ten
minutes there's someone born to take advantage of him.")

The stone that caused all the ruckus is 31 inches high by 16 inches wide by 6 inches thick, weighs 202 pounds, and now sits in the Runestone Museum in Alexandria. It was found in 1898 by Olof Ohman, who had been born in Sweden and farmed near Kensington. It wasn't until 1907 that the first complete translation from rune to English was made, by a graduate student from the University of Wisconsin named Hjalmer R. Holand:

8 Goths and 22 Norwegians on exploration journey from Vinland over the West We had camp by 2 skerries one days journey north from this stone We were and fished one day After we came home found 10 men red with blood and dead Ave Maria Save from evil.

Linguists, archaeologists, runologists, geochemists, historians, and just about everyone with an opinion has jumped in on one side or the other, and then in the summer of 2001 a team of seven called the Kensington Runestone Scientific Testing Team created a real buzz when they discovered a second stone, this one called the AVM stone for three letters inscribed thereon. We called the museum in Alexandria to find out where that stone is now and were told that several graduate students of Germanic Philology had called and admitted they had carved the inscription. And on and on it goes, and Olof's neighbor Walter Gram's deathbed confession to his grown children, saying that he helped Olof carve the runes, is pretty much ignored by everyone; especially by old Norwegians, who will stand and look at the stone for long silent moments until one finally says: "Yep. Them boys was here." The others will nod in solemn agreement.

But whatever your own take on it is, there is a large and fine statue of Big Ole, representing Scandinavians in general, standing in the main street of Alexandria just in front of the museum.

The original stone rests at the Runestone Museum, 206 Broadway, Alexandria, MN 56308. Phone (320) 763-3160.

BROKEN DOWN DAM

In 1909 Ben Snyder was the head dynamo man at the new city electrical dam on the Otter Tail River east of Fergus Falls. At 4:20 A.M. on September 24 he woke to the sound of water splashing. He jumped up, grabbed his clothes, looked out, and saw the river up at platform level. The lights were fading. He and coworker N. P. Johnson hit the door of the powerhouse at the same time the floor buckled and a ten-ton dynamo sank through it. They scrambled up the riverbank as the entire powerhouse disappeared in a torrent of black water, and after the building went down the dam itself burst apart at the center. Describing their run up the bank, Snyder said: "You could have played cards on my shirttail."

They climbed the hill above the railroad tracks and ran to the nearest farm, where Ed Burau hitched up his team and they headed into town. They met the city electrical superintendent on the way, coming out to find out why the lights had gone out. They all got to town in time to warn the citizens, as the whole reservoir of water came roaring down through the valley and took out four more dams, picking up force and debris with each one. The wreckage piled against the pier of the Mount Faith Avenue bridge and brought it down. Workers got to the Dayton Hollow dam at 6:15 A.M., just in time to open the floodgates, and it withstood the pounding.

It was the city's worst flood. Word had it that the dam had been built on a spring and that instead of providing an escape tube they simply plugged it over with concrete. The spring washed that new dam away from underneath, and once she started to go it was all over.

It's a beautiful and peaceful place, the Broken Down Dam site. Huge wedges of concrete sit strewn around like the ruins of a Roman fortress; you stand on the abutment and mentally try to reassemble the pieces. For years it was a favorite picnic spot. People would hike east along the track past the Hoot Lake Power Station carrying baskets. At night it was a place to party. Now it sits largely forgotten; there's a whole generation in town who never go out there.

A bold idea from the dam engineer: "Let's build it on a spring."

The river glides innocently through the wreckage, lapping at the big white blocks, widening itself in a shady relaxed pool just downstream. It looks too beautiful to be throwing concrete around; or, you figure, even if it could smash powerhouses and shove dams aside, it'd never do it. It's just not the type.

To get to the Broken Down Dam Park, take Interstate 94 to Minnesota Highway 210; follow MN 210 north then east. When you come to 229th Avenue take a left (north) and follow 229th until it turns into Main Street heading west. Watch for Broken Down Dam Road on your right. You may have to ask for directions, but the people are friendly.

TURTLE RACES
Longville

L ongville sits at the junction of Minnesota Highway 84 and
County Road 54; or you can drive up to Hackensack and
take County Road 5 east for 18 scenic miles. It's on Girl Lake,
within easy reach of about fifty other lakes. With apologies to
Canterbury Downs, Longville is to Minnesota what Louisville is
to Kentucky: the longtime racing center. It's been declared by
the state legislature as the Turtle Racing Capital of the World
so you know it's authentic.

There is a lot of racing in this state, primarily staged with
critters that not only can't run but also won't walk a straight
line. We generally avoid contests between trained mammals,
preferring wood ticks, frogs, box elder bugs, turtles, turkeys,
and the like. They do race Dachshunds down there in the Cities,
but speedy and graceful mammalian racing is pretty much confined to Canterbury and the county fairs. And the state prefers
the circular field to the racing oval; it places greater demands
on the judges, because the athletes all start in the middle and
the first one to clear the outside circle is the winner and it's a
tough call for a judge if they're on opposite sides.

Wednesday is Race Day. They've had afternoon racing on
Main Street here for thirty-five years, June through August, a
tradition that draws throngs of children as well as seasoned
race fans. The street is closed at 12:30 and the Turtle Mobile is
trundled out near the track—a 15-foot circle painted on the
pavement. The racing is done in heats of eight to ten turtles,
where the winner gets a white ribbon and moves on to the
finals; a green ribbon goes to the winner in the Slowpoke category, for the turtle that ends up nearest the starting point.
They go to the Slowpoke final, where the grand winner is the

Some are just born with racing in their blood.

one that moved the least. There are twenty-two volunteers who help run the event; we assume one is a veterinarian who determines that no dead, drugged, moribund, or chronically depressed turtles are registered into the competition.

If you don't own a mud turtle at least 4 inches in diameter, for a buck or two you can rent one at any number of vendors' kiosks, set up along with the registration kiosk and the memorabilia kiosk and all the other kiosks. There are peripheral games and contests going on—Turtle Golf and Turtle Hoops, Fishing for Fun, and so forth. The town population doubles on

Race Day, to about 400, and there are about as many turtles in town as people. A local woman has a racing stable of a hundred, mostly rescued from the roads around there, where they nightly risk their all just to get to some other lake.

Racing starts with the first heat at 2:00 P.M. sharp; the racers are held in the center circle by their handlers until the starter hollers "Go!" and then they're off. And the screaming and shouting start, and kids get down there along the finish circle with ice cream and call to their turtles by name.

After a hard day's racing, they award the prizes and pack it all up until the following week, just like at any other racetrack.

The races take place every Wednesday from June through August. Call the Longville Lakes Area Chamber of Commerce at (218) 363–2099 for information.

VIKING SHIP
Moorhead

The exhibition hall at the Hjemkomst Center is of a goodly size, larger than a typical church, and the big wooden sailing ship fills it right up. One wonders, diving immediately into the trivial, if this is a ship-in-the-bottle trick here or did they build ship first and hall second.

It began in 1971 when a junior high guidance counselor named Robert Asp began talking with his brother Bjarne about building a Viking ship and sailing it to Norway; a year in research and planning followed, and then Bob went searching for trees. He found white oak up by East Grand Forks and hauled it to Harvey Enden's sawmill north of Viking, where it was cut into plank, or strakes, 8 inches wide and an inch or two thick. The ends were sealed and it was sorted and left to dry for two years.

To Norway and back in a ship designed a thousand years ago.

They converted the old Leslie Welter potato warehouse in Hawley into a shipyard; tore out the first floor and built the boat in the basement, 6 feet down from street level. The 11,000 board feet of lumber and the shipyard were ready in 1974 and construction began on the keel and hull, and the work became a tourist attraction. The hull is different from modern ships in that the ribs are not rigid: strakes are riveted first to the keel and then one upon another and the ribs are fastened later, through waterproof rope connections, so that the shell is flexible, able to ride the roughest seas without breaking up. It's 76 feet long, 17 feet across, and 7 feet high at the low point. The mast can be raised and lowered so the boat can be rowed up rivers. It is a truly amazing piece of engineering from AD 890.

Six years later the front wall of the Hawley Shipyard was torn down, the sidewalk ripped out, and they began hauling gravel in for the ramp. A week later, July 17, 1980, they winched the hull up on its rollers and out into daylight; a photo from the opposite roof shows a gigantic canoe with high dramatic prows at either end, stretching all the way across the street, surrounded by figures the size of gophers.

They staged a three-day celebration, Viking Ship Days, and raised $35,000 for a voyage to Norway; Bob's mother-in-law, Hannah Foldoe, christened the ship the *Hjemkomst* on July 20. The word means "welcome" in Norwegian, pronounced *yem-komst*. It left for Duluth on August 5 and they hoisted sail for her maiden voyage on August 9; Bob took his last voyage on September 27 and died two days after Christmas, of leukemia. The family was committed to sail her to Norway.

And they did that, leaving in May 1982 with a crew of twelve including three sons and a daughter, under a mainsail of 30 by 40 feet and a topsail measuring 10 by 30, out the Great Lakes and around the Statue of Liberty and on across the stormy Atlantic, a fabulous adventure noted around the world, landing 6,000 miles later, on August 9, to a heroes' welcome in Bergen. They were greeted by the king of Norway himself.

They proved it could be done; their ancestors could have, and did, come across the Atlantic 500 years before the Spaniards. And you can see that same beautiful ship in Moorhead, where they built the hall first, rolled the hull in, and then hoisted the sails.

The Hjemkomst Interpretive Center is at 202 1st Avenue North, Moorhead 56560. Call (218) 299–5511 or visit www.hjemkomst-center.com for more information.

CORDWOOD PETE

*C*ordwood Pete was a real man, a short and fearless lumber-jack who literally did become a legend in his own time. His name was Peter DeLang. He stood 4 feet, 9 inches according to most estimates and weighed something around a hundred pounds, but he could work alongside men twice his size and more. He held his own in the taverns after work, the places that made it possible to do that North Country kind of labor day after day, and would challenge anyone who looked at him the wrong way. Fosston was a rough spot in those days, the jumping-off place from the prairie into the forest, a town full of saloons and hotels and all the rest of it; hard to picture that now on the quiet main street with the grain elevators in the background, but it was no place for the faint of heart back in the early 1900s.

Arvid Clementson with a carved likeness of Peter DeLang.

Pete built such a reputation that when the Paul Bunyan legend arose near the end of the boom days in the logging business, people began to promote Cordwood as Paul's younger brother, from back there in Bangor, Maine. He had a donkey named Tamarack, and his personality and build made him a natural counterbalance to the giant with the blue ox. Not everyone was pleased to go along with the idea of turning this real person into the brother of a fictional character. To some it just didn't sit right, but legends are legends, no matter how they get started, and most think old Pete wouldn't mind.

Pete lived to be eighty-four years old, spending his last years in a small cabin in Hill River Township. He is buried in Rose Hill Cemetery in east Fosston; the cabin and furnishings were recently donated to the Heritage Center by the Lowell Sundeen family. The Heritage Center is easily found on the main street of Fosston. The center is open May 31 through Labor Day, Friday through Sunday, 1:00 to 4:00 P.M. For more information call (218) 435–6136.

GREAT AMERICAN THINK-OFF
New York Mills

It's not exactly made-for-TV drama, even though it's been broadcast on C-SPAN; they debate the great late-night issues that have been debated by country philosophers for decades, only without all the beer. Beer lends a passion and urgency to such questions as "Does God Exist?" that is often missing in the cold crystal light of logical discussion, set before a polite audience; still, people who've watched the Think-Off say it's quite the deal. It's drawn attention from NBC, *Smithsonian* magazine, the *Baltimore Sun*, the *New York Times*, and the *Christian Science Monitor*.

New York Mills is a town of 972 sitting on the old main road between Fargo and the Twin Cities, U.S. Highway 10; it's 45 miles north of the new main road, Interstate 94. They have a good-sized Lund Boat factory there, and they have the New York Mills Regional Cultural Center, which figured they were in as good a place as any for this sort of thing. In 1993 they hosted the first Great American Think-Off, the subject of which was "The Nature of Humankind: Inherently Good or Inherently Evil?" The finalists were a priest, a newspaper editor, a fifteen-year-old cheerleader, and a tribal police officer. They debated so well the audience couldn't decide; it was a hung audience. The issue is unresolved to this day.

Four finalists are picked from hundreds of entries, from all fifty states and some foreign countries; you send in a 750-word essay and you state your opinion and back it up with personal experience, and you come prepared to debate. The Final Four get $500 plus travel and lodging. Gold, silver, and bronze medals are awarded; with the gold goes the title of America's Greatest Thinker, at least until next year.

They address burning questions long discussed by amateurs in tavern booths, such as "Does Life Have Meaning?" (the 1994 audience found that it does) and "Is Honesty Always the Best Policy?" (the 1998 audience judged not). Definitive answers to questions like these are seldom settled in the presence of pitchers of lager—where no winners are declared nor medals handed out—but in any venue healthy debate is considered a good thing, and the bedrock of a functioning democracy. Which was itself the subject of the 2000 debate, where the question was "Is Democracy Fair?" and the audiences, both in the arena and on-line, voted that it is. That winner was a suburban environmental studies teacher named Peter Hilts. Check the Web site for others. And for your entry blank.

The Think-Off is held every June. For more information write Think-Off, P.O. Box 246, New York Mills 56567; call (218) 385–3339; or visit www.think-off.org.

THE LAST ONE-ROOM SCHOOLHOUSE
Northwest Angle

The last one-room schoolhouse in Minnesota sits on the northernmost piece of land in the contiguous forty-eight states, connected to us only by water; geographically it's a peninsula but politically it's an island, and how odd for a state locked in the center of the continent to have an offshore island up in Canada.

We've always understood the reason for this was a surveying error by a crew waking up hung over and setting off ninety degrees out of whack. The truth is, as usual, more complex, having to do with border negotiations in the Treaty of Paris with the British in 1783. The British said the boundary was to

follow the Rainy River to the northwest point of Lake of the
Woods and then west to the Mississippi, not knowing at the
time that the Mississippi doesn't start in Canada. It was eighty-
nine years before they settled on a vertical stretch of border
lopping off the Angle and some outlying islands and putting
them in Minnesota.

The school has twelve grades available but in 2002 only the
first, second, third, and fifth were in use, by nine students.
There's a computer for each one, class size is real small, and
nobody comes up short on their learning. Some ride snowmobiles to school in winter and take boats in spring and fall.
When the ice is unsafe, they'll put in at one of the local resorts,
and Linda Kastl, the teacher, will sometimes sleep on the floor
of the school.

The Angle is 150 square miles of mostly national forest,
accessible by air or water or by a road cut through 45 miles of
Manitoba swamps and woods; one uses a videophone in a shack
by the road to clear Canadian customs. Life there is peaceful
but not without complexities, especially as regards conflicts in
U.S. and Canadian fishing and hunting laws. And in 1945 the
feds gave up on homesteading the place out and put it all
under the care of the Red Lake Indian Band.

So you need Canadian approval to drive to it but it's part of
the Red Lake Indian Reservation and is also under U.S. Forest
Service jurisdiction; plus it's in the Warroad School District.
Most residents think it's worth that to live in such a pristine
wilderness, on a huge lake with 14,000 islands, with great
fishing, great birding, plentiful wildlife, and historic Fort St.
Charles nearby. A lot of kids have less interesting places to go
to school.

Visit Angle Inlet School at www.yahooey.com/angleschool/
index.htm. For visitor information call or write Northwest
Angle & Island Chamber, P.O. Box 54, Oak Island, MN 56741;
call (800) 434-8531; or visit www.lakeofthewoodsresorts.com.

LAKE WOBEGON

*I*t's far and away the best-known small town in the state and many claim to have seen it, though no one seems to have found anything there interesting enough to photograph. The railroad quit its line into the place years ago, and a surveying error combined with an unfortunate position in the exact corner in a crease of the map have made it tough for travelers to locate.

It's somewhere in corn and dairy country and the residents, as near as we can tell, are pretty much like rural people in the rest of the state: stubborn, resistant to change, and given to the occasional practical joke but perhaps not quite so much as their ancestors were. And of course churchgoing and practical, at least most of the time. It's a place best read and heard about from a distance; if you were actually to find yourself there you'd face the possibility of a letdown, disappointed by its everyday nature and by how closely the residents resemble your own relatives. You might be so struck by it all as to forget even how to give directions to the place.

Lake Wobegon is best explored through the works of the distinguished American writer Garrison Keillor, who claims to have been a resident—although he also once claimed to be "a professional liar." Few would challenge either claim.

POULTRY MUSEUM
Pine River

Loyl Stromberg grew up in the poultry trade, in the Stromberg Hatchery in Fort Dodge, Iowa; they were a force in the chicken business for forty years, until the big egg factories came along. He's eighty-seven and lives on Upper Whitefish Lake, on the site of the family's old summer cabin, and he's still in the family enterprise, now called Stromberg's Chicks and Gamebirds Unlimited. His card reads:

> If an old man likes a young girl,
> *That's his business!*
> And if a young girl likes an old man,
> *That's her business!*
> And if they want to get married,
> *That's their business!*
> And if you look on the other side,
> *That's our business!*

On the back, of course, is the address and phone number, the business description and a list of Stromberg Books, including *Making Squab Raising Profitable* and *Swan Breeding and Management,* and *Dubbing Poultry and Why*—and who hasn't wondered why—plus *Caponizing, Management & Profitable Marketing.* He also wrote *Sexing All Fowl, Gamebirds & Cage Birds* and *Poultry Oddities, History and Folklore.* And if you've been thinking your front lawn might look good with a big colorful peacock on it, read his *Pea Fowl Breeding & Management.* Altogether he's written fourteen books on poultry. The latest is the penultimate *Poultry of the World,* which has 396 pages and was seventeen years in the writing (actually longer than the book you are now holding).

Stromberg's mail-order catalog is an amazing document in itself—they sell books, brooders, incubators, caponizers, and all that other gear, plus eggs, chicks, and breeders in a boggling variety of birds: twenty-nine varieties of ducks, including the Chiloe Wigeon and the Falcated Teal; ten breeds of geese, including Barheads, Barnacles, Lesser Snows, and Giant Canadas; ten pheasants, including the Satyr Tragopan, the Lady Amherst, the Impeyan, and Temminck's Tragopan. They show all kinds of quail, doves, pigeons, and turkeys; guineas, ducks, geese, peafowl; all the way up to swans, five varieties, including Black Australians, White Mute Swans ($1,000 for a young pair, $1,200 for proven breeders), and young Trumpeters at $1,500 a pair. (It's $500 extra for birds that trumpet—although after hearing them, one might pay extra for Mute.)

But the chickens: They aren't just talking Leghorns and Wyandottes here. It's Mottled Houdans, Egyptian Fayoumis, Saipan Jungle Fowl, and sixty other standard breeds. In bantams they offer the various Brahmas and Cochins, plus the Blue Mille Fleur d'Uccle, the White-crested Black Polish, the Silver Duckwing Old English, and the Feather Legged White Frizzle, and about a hundred others as well.

Still, the real stunner is his amazing museum. There are chicken statues, chicken bric-a-brac, chicken paintings covering every wall of home and office. Chicken sculptures from mundane to elegant. Chickens of blown glass, of jade, of carved exotic wood. Stuffed chickens, including a pair of fighting cocks in battle. Chicken likenesses of every nationality: Russian, Spanish, German, Japanese, Chinese—from everywhere—thousands, and Loyl can tell you the origin of every one.

He has collected equipment from around the world as well and is the prime mover behind the new National Poultry Museum in Kansas.

Donations are welcome and are tax deductible. Send contributions to National Poultry Museum, 630 Hall of Fame Drive, Bonner Springs, KS 66012.

A plethora of chickenalia awaits you at the
National Poultry Museum.

For a catalog write Stromberg's Chicks and Gamebirds
Unlimited, P.O. Box 400, Pine River, MN 56474; call (800)
720–1134 or (218) 587–2222; or visit www.strombergschickens.
com. To see Loyl's collection in Minnesota, contact him at 8302
Big Whitefish Narrows, Pine River, MN 56474, or phone him at
(218) 543–4228.

SIN CITY

The Fargo-Moorhead visitor bureau says their metropolis has one of the lowest crime rates in the nation, but it wasn't always that way, especially from 1878 to 1915. Will Rogers once called Moorhead "the wickedest city in the world." He was a humorist and given to embellishment, of course, and it's hard to imagine Moorhead in a league with Tangiers, Tijuana, Rio de Janeiro, or Singapore, or even London at that time; but Moorhead did pretty darn good for a little town way out there on the frozen plain.

The Law of Unintended Consequences was partly in play there, and so was the Law of Intended Consequences: Fargo, North Dakota, allowed easy divorce—ten minutes—because they were generally hardworking practical folks who felt that being in a bad marriage was miserable enough without having to go through a big rigmarole to get out of it, and they also were a dry state at the time so you couldn't go out and drink afterward. You were supposed to go right back to work. Folks across the river in Moorhead knew an opportunity when they saw it, and saloon-keeping became a big industry in a hurry.

There were dozens of them, and they didn't go at it in a half-hearted way, either. One, the Higgins-Aske Co., had three eight-drawer cash registers, an enormously long bar, and tile floors; another boasted of 400 electric lights; Rustad's had inlaid brass footsteps in the sidewalk leading to their door, and the White House had an outdoor summer garden and a functioning electric fountain inside.

And they didn't just sit and wait for clients. They'd send out wagons; some would go over to Fargo and bring patrons back free, while others would actually go out into farm fields and sell shots of whiskey to the hands working there. Farmers' hearts would sink in the middle of a harvest afternoon to see that wagon show up.

But when you stay up late and you've got gambling and all those women dressed in silk coming in there, and there's all kinds of money floating around—in other words, when you start having too much fun—you just know it can't last. The whole thing got run underground by do-gooders in 1915 when they voted Clay County dry. Moonshine was made there in basements through Prohibition, just as it was in every city in the nation; but at least for a while Moorhead had style and opulence, and the honor of being a famously wicked place.

TANK RIDE
Princeton

The Tank Ride camp sits like a small military outpost in farm country; basically a shallow gravel pit with a couple of old trailer houses near a pond. The overpowering presence of a Russian tank dominates the center of the hard-pack yard, thirty tons of menace, the cannon leveled east toward the tree line. Farther off, against the bluff to the north, is a pistol range where half a dozen police cars sit while their operators take a firearms course. Historian and mechanical wizard Bob Bowman comes out of the trailer to greet us in the manner of a man hosting a party, smiling, glad we could make it.

He describes our various duties—gunner, commander, or machine gunner, himself the driver—and gives us some background. This one was built in 1944, eventually captured by the German Viking Division, ended its war in Poland, painted with German field gray and iron crosses over the Russian green. The T-34 was the best in the world; the Germans were happy to grab them whenever they could and paint them over. (The tanks didn't care; they were all neutral.) Bob bought it from the Polish government. It's the only one in the United States in running order and accessible to the public.

What made these tanks the best—a German general once said, "This tank adversely affected the morale of the German infantry"—was not sophistication but logic: sloped armored sides, low profile, rear engine/rear drive (all others had rear engine/front drive), a big-wheel carriage with wide tracks (they wouldn't freeze solid with mud and they didn't get stuck), compressed-air starting, and an overall simplicity that allowed them to be repaired in the field by soldiers who had never driven a car, never seen a flush toilet or a lightbulb. There were no hydraulics or power assists; the gunner rotated the turret and elevated the gun with hand cranks, and the driver steered by the sheer strength of his arms and legs.

We don the coveralls, padded leather helmets, and goggles, then climb aboard. Bob fires it up; the twelve-cylinder diesel has an amazing roar. We set off across the lot into the battlefield, through deep mud holes and up and along the steep base of the bluff. We recall movies of these things flying along raising sand, looking smooth as limos, and we had no idea; once inside, it seems built for maximum utilitarian misery, like a race car.

But it's also exhilarating, an incredible carnival ride through brutal reality, rough and jolting, pitching, nose-diving over ledges, grinding and howling up over the crest of a ridge, coming face to face with a cannon in the trees. It fires at us, a bright blast and a loud explosion; our gunner cranks desperately to bring the turret over; he lowers to find it in the eyepiece and the cannon fires a second time, and we fire back, KABOOM. The guns are lit off Hollywood style, with oxygen and propane, but we definitely get the message.

We twist and turn and crash through the woods and find another gun, across a small pond. We stop and try to bear on it before it fires, and again we shoot second. We move on, descend a steep bluff, climb over a wrecked car, and the ride ends back at the yard all too soon; forty-five minutes we will never forget, for all kinds of reasons.

The trailer house is also the firing line of the machine-gun range, with an open bench overlooking the pond and various junk beyond. You never understand what guys see in firing machine guns until you actually do it; it's one of those things in life that are vastly more enjoyable than you ever imagined, like lovemaking or fancy desserts. Except with the machine gun you feel even more guilt, an extra bonus, for finding delight in such a harsh undertaking.

On a scale from 1 to 5, we give the incredible Tank Ride 6 stars. Ladies are welcome, and they seem to enjoy it as much as the men.

Take U.S. Highway 169 north, exiting onto Minnesota Highway 95; go ½ mile west and take a right (north) onto County Road 102 for 2 miles to the TANK sign. For more information call (866) 888–TANK, visit www.tankride.com, or e-mail tankride@prodigy.net.

PRAIRIE CHICKEN

*P*rairie Chickens were once as common in Minnesota as black-
birds, of which there were millions. They were hunted, of
course, but it was all that farming that really put them out of
business. There's a strip of bluestem prairie out west of Bar-
nesville and Rothsay where they're making a comeback these
days, though, and for the few dozen folks who get out there to the
mating grounds around April 20 at dawn, they put on a spectacular show. The males gather in crowds of about forty, stake out
territories, square off, and bully each other, dancing and hopping
and inflating big orange sacs on each side of their necks, making
a three-note booming sound; females walk around among these
wild guys and act disinterested. Eventually some get interested
enough, which is why there are now 2,700 Prairie Chickens in the
state.

They weigh about two pounds apiece and are considered
tasty by those who remember the days when they were hunted;
of course those people are thinking back to 1941, the last time it
was legal. These days the meat is a secondary consideration; it's
show business that draws the fans now. Prairie Chicken is
almost too honest a name for such a fiesty and dramatic bird.
It sounds like a derogatory term someone might use for a mid-
westerner, out of his element in a bar full of longshoremen.

Rothsay was roughly the center of the Prairie Chicken population in its heyday, and there is a grand statue of a male in
full formal mating dress there. It was built of cement and steel
in a big garage by a man named Art Fosse, who spent most of
his life in the trucking business; he says he's not really a sculptor but he's got quite a shop and he's handy with a torch and
that sort of thing. It's "one of my hobbies," he adds, and the
bird was built at his suggestion. Using a mounted bird from the
university as a model, he made a steel frame and subframe,
covered it with cement and plaster, and painted it. He makes it
sound like there was nothing to it, but it weighs 9,000 pounds.
It was covered with a World War II parachute and hauled to
the site; at the big dedication in June 1976, Art says, they
removed the parachute and "there was all kinds of fanfare . . .

A 9,000-pound bird looking for a date.

radio stations and so forth." It was pictured on the front page of the Minneapolis Tribune.

It's close to the road and very photogenic, and the nearby little truck stop is not that bad of a place to get some pie and coffee.

The World's Largest Prairie Chicken stands near the east-bound exit ramp on Interstate 94 at Rothsay.

M O L E H I L L
S a u k R a p i d s

If you dream about temples rising out of rock and rubble—
and who doesn't—there is a place at 601 3rd Avenue North
in Sauk Rapids that might look familiar to you; if it's not
exactly what you dreamed of, it probably comes close in some
places.

It was built by a retired railroad man named Louis Wippich,
whose parents had come over from East Prussia in 1879. He
was born on a farm near Gilman; they moved to a vegetable
farm in Sauk Rapids in 1913. Louis left school in the fifth
grade to help his father, joined the navy in 1916, was discharged in 1919, worked as a carpenter and cement finisher
until he hired on at the railroad, from which he retired twenty-
four years later. Kind of standard upbringing for the time.
Nothing in there to suggest he would one day lose himself in
theosophical teachings of Madame H. P. Blavatsky and in 1932
begin writing and building a gigantic fantasy in stone on four
city lots.

It's a memorial to the imagination of man, the freedom of the
spirit, and the lost art of heavy lifting; even the smallest stones
weigh 1,200 pounds. Louis moved them into place with cables
and levers and the thirty-five-cents-an-hour labor of teenagers.
He built a pair of angular towers, the tallest 45 feet high, plus
a Grecian temple, a reflecting pool, a Romanesque stairway,
and a wall with seven Doric pillars standing on it, most from
leftover stone from local quarries and demolition sites. But
there are a few special pieces, like the blue granite quarried
from the bottom of a Swedish lake. There are labyrinthian passageways underneath the fantastic stone structures. He called
it the Molehill, and himself the Clown of the Molehill.

It may look like the work of an ancient culture, but Molehill was actually built in 1932 by retired railroad man Louis Wippich.

Water of course is always at war with stone, and water brings green things in to move stone and break it down, and when Louis got too old to work it became overgrown, and eventually the people in the rental house he'd built there began to use the garden for a landfill. When he died in 1973, at the age of seventy-eight, he left no will; his estate was put up for sale to the highest bidder and in 1974 a grandnephew named Donald Manea, who had played in the garden as a boy, bought it.

Donald and his wife, Alina, have worked for a long time now, first the years cleaning out all the garbage, next the years restoring the old stonework, then the years building a new stone home integral with the structures already in place. You can't describe it, and they don't offer tours. You just have to go and see it, even if you can't get inside; it's plenty dramatic from the sidewalk.

The Molehill Rock Garden is on the corner of 3rd Avenue North and 6th Street in Sauk Rapids. Take the Sauk Rapids exit off U.S. Highway 10, then turn left up 6th before the downtown. The Manea residence is at 601 3rd Avenue North.

W O R L D ' S *L A R G E S T* *L E F S E*
S t a r b u c k

It was a big year, 1983, when they celebrated the centennial of the founding of Starbuck, and they wanted to do it right. They put on a ten-day extravaganza in late June and early July, including an all-class reunion attended by Bertha Metlie Lilienthal from the first graduating class, class of 1910, along with 1,200 others who followed; and vocal concerts and band concerts, and the Pope County Dairy Princess was there to serve ice cream to the public, and an open house was held at the fire department so you could climb on the fire engines. Those who had airplanes flew in to the annual Pope County Fly-In.

They staged a Centennial Historical Pageant, a Water Fun Carnival, and a Medallion Hunt. Scandinavian crafts and food booths lined the main street. The Snoose Street Singers sang and there was Norwegian dancing and then the Swedish Singers sang, and it was quite the deal.

The highlight of the whole thing was the baking of the World's Largest Lefse. Lefse is a delicate flat potato pastry—at least my grandmother's was delicate—best served warm with butter, powdered sugar, and morning coffee. It measured 9 feet, 8 inches by 9 feet, 1 inch when it was done, larger than they had expected and a grand success. Eight men baked it using thirty-two pounds of potatoes, thirty pounds of flour, four pounds of shortening, two pounds of sugar, and twelve ounces of salt. A hay rack was used as a counter for the pastry board where they rolled the dough, using a 6-foot binder roller. A slatted roller was built to roll the flattened dough around to move it onto the griddle.

The griddle was made of two 5- by 10-foot flat plates of steel, each weighing 600 pounds, welded together to make a 10-foot square. Parallel rails were set, fifteen bags of charcoal were spread between the rails and lit, and then with log chains and pry bars they slid the griddle onto the rails. The dough was unrolled over the griddle and they stood around and judged its progress, and then eight guys in unison, using boat paddles, turned the dough over on its other side. An official measurement was taken and verified.

Getting the pastry off the hot plate was tricky but they managed, with minimal damage, and it was cut up and buttered and sugared, like it's supposed to be, and served warm to the crowd. They saved a piece for Governor Perpich and another for King Olav of Norway. We don't know if it ever reached His Majesty or not, but it did make it into the *Shipstead Book of Records,* the Norwegian equivalent to the *Guinness Book of World Records* (which didn't even have a category for giant lefse). The city still celebrates the event every summer.

Starbuck is 20 miles east of Morris on County Highway 28. For information on Lefse Dagen in Starbuck, call the chamber of commerce at (320) 239–4220.

FABULOUS BOB

It would be interesting enough to live in Motley—or Fertile, or any other place with an adjective name—just to read the newspaper captions (MOTLEY FARMER MARRIES FERTILE WOMAN; MOTLEY POLICEMAN PROMOTED; MOTLEY TEACHERS TO STRIKE; et cetera) without someone coming along and making outrageous news on their own. In this case it's a local man known as Fabulous Bob who says he "went to New York and graduated from Columbia University with a double Ph.D. in psychology and theology," and became an ordained minister in the Church of Christ.

He had disagreements with his church, feeling that they were too conservative in some ways, and when he was "somewhere between thirty-five and forty-five" he moved to New Orleans, visited the hall of the High Priestess of Voodoo, Marie LaVieux, and suddenly, as he says, "felt comfortable." He followed through with these feelings and became a High Priest of Voodoo himself, however one goes about doing that, and he ultimately moved back to his hometown where he got a regular job and then set up an altar and developed a small clientele . . . and seems to be doing just fine. He says, "People think voodoo involves the sacrifice of chickens. We do not. That is a Hollywood myth."

He's also a member of a conservative think tank and is a flamboyant dresser and doesn't see any of it as contradiction, and goes to meetings wearing whatever seems right at the moment, whether it be furs, jewelry, knickers, or sweatpants. At first people had problems with some of this, he says, but they adapt. "'It's just Bob,' they say, 'don't worry about it. It's just the way he is.'"

Fabulous Bob, bringing comfort to Voodoo-deprived Motley citizens.

None of this finds its way into the local headlines and he doesn't advertise, but it's not exactly a secret, either; if we could find him, anybody else in town could as well. He says, "You can do this in rural Minnesota, and people will adapt."

And there you have it. Motley residents adapt to voodoo priest.

Bob Jenkins lives at 281 1st Avenue South, Motley. His phone number is (218) 352–6629.

E E L P O U T   F E S T I V A L
Walker

The dictionary says this about the eelpout: "1. any fish of the family Zoarcidae, esp. *Zoarces viviparus,* of Europe." It could also have said: "2. one of the world's unique and truly ugly creatures, bringing shock, disgust, and revulsion into any boat unlucky enough to catch one." The eelpout and his family may or may not be named after Zoar, the city in the Old Testament where Lot is said to have sought refuge during the destruction of Sodom and Gomorrah, but at any rate it ranks low on most people's social ladder of fishes. It has a blunt face, bulging eyes, no scales, and smooth slimy skin like a catfish except in a splotchy brown-and-black instead of a sleek all-black. But as the name suggests, its worst aspect is a double-flex backbone that gives it the same menacing moves as a snake; all this plus a creepy little barbel on its chin. It gives some fisher-folk the nightmares.

In Walker they are buying none of this silly fearmongering; up there, they claim the eelpout to be "the only true game fish" and celebrate it every February with a three-day festival, the high point of which is an Eelpout Fishing Contest where elite teams of crack fishermen compete for prizes. Ken Bresly, the organizer, says that there are strict mental and physical examinations for the entrants before they're allowed to actually enter the contest; for instance, one of the questions on the mental exam is "What is your name?" You don't necessarily have to know your last name, but you have to at least remember your first name, or one of your names. For the physical, you have to be able to stand erect for more than thirty seconds ("we eliminate a big pile of them right there"); another requirement, for example, is that you have to be able to find your car keys. Or at least, somebody's keys ("and that's another toughie").

*A face only a mother
could love.*

He notes that contestants aren't encouraged to bring an ordinary fish to the judges: ". . . If they catch a walleye, or somethin' like that, and they bring those into the headquarters, we won't even allow that to be hung on the same *rack* that the eelpout are on. Because we don't want to contaminate the eelpout. We're real concerned about that." Asked whether, if you were to by chance catch a record walleye while you were fishing for eelpout, you'd have to not say anything about it and toss it back, Ken says, "Either that or hide it. Sneak it home and have it ground into pet food . . . in fact, you're not allowed to bring anything like that in. We have a number of people arrested each year for that very thing. Because again, they might contaminate the eelpout. We just can't take a chance on that."

We allowed as how the festival sounded like a good time and Ken said that it's possible, if you force yourself, to have a good time, but of course that's not the point of it. The point is the sport of it, the *art* of the eelpout, and to get out and become one with nature. And all that sort of thing. A person is permitted one glass of sherry before dinner, which often features Eelpout Nuggets; any more than that might blur one's palate, so as to obscure the amazing flavors of the deep-fried eelpout.

Asked if the governor has been to the festival, Ken replies, "No, but we think this is the year. You see, he's kind of a rookie. And he really doesn't want to be embarrassed. And we try not to, but . . . y'know, it's uh . . . Well, he's *good*. But he's just not *that* good, y'know, to fish for eelpout . . . We invite him every year. And we will certainly do that again this year, but . . . well, he's just never been drafted by a team, and there's gotta be a reason for that; and I don't know what that reason is. See, we have a draft every year, just *preceding* the NFL draft—and nobody's picked him up yet. But I think first we have to get him up here, because these are his people. If he came up here, I think some team would pick him up."

You fish for eelpout exactly as you fish for walleye, but certain people have their little secret baits and so forth. World-class eelpout fishermen are on hand at the tournament, going from fish house to fish house, apparently to offer tips and encouragement. The world record, as far as Ken knows, is seventeen pounds. A seventeen-pound eelpout, we thought, would be well over 2 feet long, and he says, "Yes indeed; I think it's closer to 3 feet, or maybe 4." We couldn't help but wonder if whoever caught that thing was able to sleep that night. Or even now.

The Eelpout Festival is held the third weekend of February. For more information call the Leech Lake Area Chamber of Commerce at (800) 833–1118 or (218) 547–1313 or visit www.leech-lake.com.

THE WADSWORTH TRAIL

*I*n the years following the Civil War, the Wadsworth Trail ran west from St. Cloud through Sauk Center and Glenwood and on to Fort Wadsworth in the Dakota Territory. There was a stop along the way called Gager's Station, just north of Morris, where in an unknown year between 1864 and 1871 a gentleman from the East arrived driving a team of oxen. He was a musician and had played in "a famous orchestra in the East," and had come out here for adventure. Seems like kind of a joke now, that someone would come to Minnesota from Philadelphia or New York for adventure.

His name was Albert Hawkes, his clothes were always clean and pressed, and he didn't smoke, drink, swear, or gamble; stood out like a bride in a pigsty. His sense of humor was all that saved him from being run out of town, that and his team of oxen. When he had shopped for them, he didn't care for the ordinary animals that answered only to hish, gee, and haw; he thought that far too crude. So he bought a young pair and trained them himself, teaching them to respond to square dancing commands. It became a real treat for the town when Albert would drive that team down the street and around the block, singing out "Forward all," "Gents to the right," and "Allemande left." They'd do more than just start and turn, too; they could "Promenade" and "Swing your partners" and do "Ladies forward and back."

Albert took a job driving the stagecoach from Gager's Station to Bismarck, described as a teamster's nightmare, through sinkholes and mud and along easily ambushed high ground. He made it to Bismarck and then was sent out on a newly laid trail to the Black Hills in South Dakota, where he became "one of the first drivers to be shot by Indians on that trail." They didn't say what happened to the team of oxen, but without the manual it would have been hard for anyone else to drive it.

Seems unfair, doesn't it? A clever guy, a musician, a free spirit in clean clothes out there on the muddy frontier, gunned down by people who just didn't give him a chance to show them his talent or his humorous side. If there's a moral to the story it would be something like this: In hostile territory, wit is less valuable than having someone along to ride shotgun.

UFO COLLIDES WITH SHERIFF'S PATROL CAR
Warren

All the elements are here: the lone eyewitness an honest, well-respected small-town deputy sheriff whose credibility had never been questioned, knocked cold at the scene; the actual damage on the patrol car caused by an unknown object; the bright flash of light so intense it injured the deputy's retinas for a time; and the mysterious simultaneous stopping of two clocks, one mechanical and one electrical, for fourteen minutes. All this followed by a visit from an investigator sent by UFO headquarters in Indiana.

At 1:30 A.M. on August 27, 1979, Marshall County Deputy Val Johnson was headed west from Stephen on County Road 5. Approaching Minnesota Highway 220 he saw a light to the south that looked like it might be a light plane in trouble about 2 miles away. He turned south onto MN 220; the light seemed to hang there and then suddenly came right down the road at him, he said, fast and bright. There was a crash. He was knocked cold and came to forty minutes later, remembering the sound of breaking glass and nothing more. He called for help on the radio, saying he'd been hit by something but it wasn't a vehicle. He didn't know what it was.

The car traveled 854 feet from the point of impact to the place where the brakes were applied, and then it skidded 99 feet and ended up crosswise on the road. It had a broken headlight, a dent on the hood, a broken windshield, and a damaged red light on the roof. Two spring-mounted antennae were bent sharply backward, and the clock was running fourteen minutes slow. There was no evidence of another vehicle anywhere within a mile. Deputy Johnson had a bump on his head, apparently from hitting the steering wheel, and his eyes hurt from "welder's burn." And his watch was fourteen minutes slow.

When it hit the paper, a number of other people came forward to report similar incidents in that area but none had made actual contact with a bright object; investigations looked into the case but no solid conclusions were drawn. Johnson himself still says he doesn't know what it was; it's a mystery to this day. The sheriff at the time, Dennis Brekke, said, "We've had something here and we really don't know what it is. I'm not reporting that we believe in flying saucers or don't believe in flying saucers. What he's [Johnson] seen, he's seen. None of us are trained to explain things we're not used to seeing."

But because it drew national attention at the time, the patrol car was never repaired; it sits now on display in the Marshall County Museum in Warren. People around the area still wonder about it. There are many theories.

Warren is located 31 miles north of Crookston on U.S. Highway 75. To see the UFO Car call the Marshall County Historical Society at (218) 478–2743 or (218) 745–4031.

SUPERMAN

His real name is John. He's a big guy and he's in St. Cloud and he's fighting against evil and for the American way. He wears a Superman costume, stands 6 feet, 3 inches tall and weighs 265 and then some, most of it muscle, and he works in construction. His shoulders are wide as a pickup truck and his arms are big as most of our legs. He's had some experiences he doesn't care to talk about that have driven him to stand near heavy traffic in a cape, hold a flag, wave, smile, and represent "the collective will and the common good." A larger-than-life character who says that 90 percent of the people in St. Cloud are good people but 10 percent need to change their evil ways and it's his purpose to stand out there and fight crime and bad attitudes by setting an example and being a living symbol. Courage-challenged college kids razz him when they drive by but not when they walk by. Most people wave.

He told a reporter: "I live here, and strange mysterious events have prompted me to wear the costume. St. Cloud is in desperate need of a super hero." He sees Superman as the symbol of truth and justice. He's standing up against evil, same as the real Superman. And for a small fee, you can have your picture taken with him; the money goes to travel expenses, when he goes to other towns or to the state fair.

He can be seen in warm weather near the St. Cloud Law Enforcement Center, the Dairy Queen, or the Crossroads Center mall; you won't need binoculars.

You can contact St. Cloud Superman at www.Stcloudsuperman.com.

A man does what a man's gotta do.

NORTHEAST

NORTHEAST

FISH HOUSES ON PARADE
Aitkin

They hold the parade on the Friday after Thanksgiving, someone said, "to not distract everybody away from Macy's." Someone else said, "There's not many in northern Minnesota who much care about Macy's—it's just that we don't have a mall, so why not watch fish houses go by? Gotta be more fun than shopping anyway."

And it seems to be. They drew 6,000 spectators in 2001, their eleventh year, and were expecting even more in November 2002. Another one of those cold celebrations that the media seem drawn to like mosquitoes to a baby, or more like frost to a windshield. They've been in *USA Today* and a number of newspapers from the warmer latitudes, like Dallas; in 2001 Comedy Central brought their own float, along with a camera crew.

There are prizes: Most Creative, Most Humorous, Noisiest (lots of racket before that long winter silence sets in), Best Fish House, and Best Youth Entry. Some have bands, some have boom boxes, some have walkers alongside tossing candy; they all have a fish house, or a suggestion of one. We figured if we entered a fish house we'd build it invisible: all mirrors, inside and out, and set diagonally on the trailer. (Go ahead and win a prize with our idea, somebody; we just don't have the time.)

The floats gather at the fairgrounds at noon and the parade starts at 1:00 P.M., goes for eight blocks, and then the awards

Hollywood in the North Woods.

The world's draftiest igloo.

A fish finder, finding fish.

are given out at City Hall. Bathroom humor was a popular theme when the event was younger—a guy fishing out of a toilet was big hit—but they've moved onward and upward to wacky costumes, igloos, Jaws, hot tubs, fish finders, a dog with antlers, the Crappie Queen, celebrities and athletes, plus every fire engine the town ever owned. All this and an American Legion Chili Cook-Off, the bank's Fish House Stew at the Moose Lodge, and pancake breakfasts and sloppy joe lunches.

You don't see the skin you see at Mardi Gras and Aitkin isn't quite the French Quarter, but they do have a party spirit up here.

Contact Aitkin Chamber of Commerce, 12 2nd Street Northwest, Aitkin, MN 56431; (218) 927–2316 or (800) 526–8342.

ICE DIVING

Minnesota *is variously translated as "stands in canoe," "falls into water," or "drops things in lake." Bill Matthies has been diving in the North Country for more than forty years; the lake and river bottoms yield a steady twenty snowmobiles and three cars every winter, plus a broad range of other valuables, from wedding rings—they slip off cold fingers—up to D7 Caterpillar tractors, two of which sank in 20 feet of mud near Randall. Bill uses an underwater metal detector if the bottom is soft, but is generally able to see what he's looking for down there. He's pulled up boats, fishing tackle, guns, airplanes, trucks, slot machines, and ninety-nine unfortunate persons.*

Last year a man was ice fishing on Mille Lacs Lake as part of an American Legion steak fry; somehow his upper plate fell out and dropped through the hole. He wore a ski mask the rest of the day so people couldn't see what he looked like without his teeth. They called Bill and he put a float in the hole with a weight set to ride a foot off the bottom. Then he sawed a bigger hole nearby, went down, and found the teeth right where they were supposed to be, under the weight, and the man had steak that night. It's not uncommon to find teeth, Bill says; one pictures lakebeds strewn with upper plates.

Besides the recovery business he also teaches; he says the first tool of ice divers is a snow shovel. They clear a patch of ice and then shovel pathways radiating out from the center. They cut a triangular hole with a chain saw and from below the pathways create a bright illumination, "like a big fluorescent light up there." They lower themselves into a bluegreen world, cold and wet and luminous, with this amazing brilliance streaming down.

The favorite waters of the recreational diver are the old mine pits of the Cuyuna Range, where the water is crystal pure and you can see for 100 feet. The terraced landscape is a fantasy of steep cliffs, old shacks, tun-

Thin ice is one of nature's ways to cull the herd.

nels, power lines, and railroad beds. Fish move in the trees
down there, and in spring eelpout wrap themselves around
branches and lay eggs. Loons come down to cruise among the
divers; an odd symbiosis, human and bird, swimming underwater. One pit is more ghostly yet; swimming near a bare-
branch woods, you make out what looks like a far-off pale
skeleton hanging from a tree and find to your horror that it
is. Farther on another sits grinning in a chair, legs crossed,
and yet another slumps against a power pole, bone fingers
gripping two bare wires from a fusebox. A gigantic Jurassic
turtle, 8 feet across, lies on the bottom like a musty sunken
UFO. This lake draws crowds of divers.

If being underwater in a freezing cold mine-pit lake with
2 feet of solid ice between yourself and the real world is your
idea of a good time, you will find yourself in good company
on the Cuyuna Range. And you'd better bring your sense of
humor, because there are jokers among them.

Minnesota School of Diving is located at 712 Washington
Street in Brainerd. Call (800) OK–SCUBA or (218) 829–5953
for information, or visit www.mndiving.com.

THE TRUE CANOE
Bigfork

In an age when cheap quartz watches are more accurate than anything ever made by hand, there are still certain instruments of which the best can be built only by ancient methods. Violins, for instance. And canoes.

Canoeists generally agree that birch bark is superior to aluminum and fiberglass: it's lighter, stronger, more flexible, easier to repair; most importantly, it's easier to paddle, quieter in the water, and it *feels* better. It has spirit. But they aren't manufactured; they're handmade and lashed together without fasteners. One of the few places in the world where they take the time to do this is the Hafeman Boat Works in Bigfork, now run by Ray Boessel Jr.

Bill Hafeman and his wife, Violet, homesteaded here in 1920 and faced a 7-mile weekly hike to town for supplies; the river offered an easier way. Bill learned how to build canoes using age-old Indian methods, built from the outside in, with bark from birch trees, white cedar strips for the ribs, black spruce roots for the binding, pitch and bear grease for sealant. Canoes like this were used by the Natives and by French traders to travel the Great Lakes. The big ones, 37 feet long and 5 feet wide, could carry more than three tons of cargo and fourteen men. They were called the *canot du maître,* the Montreal canoe, and they were the mainstay of the fur trade in the North in the 1700s. Not a single old one survives today, because nobody ever thought of putting one in a museum. Most of the few in existence were built by Hafeman Boat Works.

Bill became a legend as a woodsman and boatbuilder; he built about six a year for sixty years. His canoes were of all sizes and became known worldwide, and famous people like

Ray Boessel Jr. and a rack of future national treasures.

Lady Bird Johnson bought them. Two of his apprentices are still helping to keep the tradition alive; one of these is Ray Boessel Jr., married to Bill Hafeman's granddaughter Christie.

Ray makes ten to fifteen canoes a year; each begins as a long search through the woods, and most are spoken for before they're built. He builds them in the various styles; the shape of the ends identifies the tribe of origin. He's made 252 canoes in twenty-two years, including the big ones, and he's not optimistic about the future of the birch canoe, mostly because of the difficulty of finding large enough birch trees and the recent efforts to stop the taking of even small amounts of cedar.

LIGHTHOUSES

A lot of states have soybean fields and quite a few others have lighthouses but Minnesota is one of the rare places that have both; it's not a significant relationship—the lights never burned soybean oil—but it's an oddity relating to this deep-water seaport we have here in the middle of the continent.

The stretch of Lake Superior shoreline between Two Harbors and Split Rock was considered one of the most dangerous waters in the world. A storm in 1905 wrecked twenty-nine ships in two days, most of them belonging to U.S. Steel, and they pressured Congress for some warning lights and foghorns, and they got them. The fundamental problem was the huge deposits of iron ore beneath the lake, which mess up navigational compasses; being caught in a winter storm at night with no compass was many a sailor's nightmare finish.

The lighthouses are no longer needed in the age of radar, depth finders, and global positioning, but they make excellent tourist attractions; the one in Two Harbors is a bed-and-breakfast and the one at Split Rock is just a beautifully proportioned and dramatically situated famous building.

Contact Lighthouse Bed & Breakfast, 1 Lighthouse Point, P.O. Box 313, Two Harbors 55616; (218) 834–4898 or (888) 832–5606.

Split Rock Lighthouse is roughly 20 miles north of Two Harbors on Minnesota Highway 61; there are signs. The phone number is (218) 226–6377. It's open only in summer.

So if you've always wanted to own a Stradivarius but can't quite afford it, you might consider a canoe with 500 years of history, made by Ray Boessel Jr.

Hafeman Boat Works is located 30 miles straight north of Deer River on County Road 6 where it intersects with the Big Fork River. Contact Hafeman Boat Works, Rural Route 1, Box 187, Bigfork 56628. Call (218) 743–3709 if you get lost.

BASSHENGE
Birchdale

It began as one of those "Why Not?" moments between couples. In the summer of 1999 Joe Gaustefeste, who has been with the Chicago Symphony forty-one years and is their principal bassist, was sitting with his wife, writer Yvette Journeau, watching a National Geographic special on TV about Stonehenge. She turned to him and said, "Why not a Basshenge?"

An innocent question he couldn't answer, and on the Fourth of July 2001, set in a clef-shaped walkway near the Rainy River, twenty-one steel basses stood tall on twenty-one concrete pedestals. To a passerby they imply there could be more here than meets the eye, and there is.

They already had the land, eighty acres and a cabin west of International Falls, near Birchdale. (Chicago used to stash gangsters in the North Country but now they're sending classical musicians; considered an improvement, in many ways.) Joe was born in Brooklyn, where they raise people who like to get things done, and through his work he had connections to artists and sculptors. He decided on ⅜-inch ordinary plate steel as the medium; they would be of three different styles abstracted from the three clefs in which the bass is played—

Seven sins and seven virtues—music, art, and history in
⅜-inch steel plate.

bass, tenor, and treble—designed by himself, sculptor Richard
Hunt, and puppet maker Mathew Owens. Ten lintels would
span between the eighteen 6-foot basses, and three 10-foot
basses would stand in the center, all on 5-foot pedestals.

The lintels were designed from images by painter Sam Agres
of the seven virtues—prudence, temperance, justice, fortitude,
faith, hope, and charity—overlaid on images of the seven
deadly sins—covetousness, pride, lust, anger, gluttony, sloth,
and greed. Three other lintels represent arcane musical con-
cepts, like harmony, conflict, and brotherhood.

The pedestals are 16 inches in diameter and 14 feet tall—9 of
these feet are below ground—and because the soft ground
couldn't support a cement truck they all had to be hand-
poured. Leland Nelson cut the steel, his brother Ralph did the
surveying, and Eugene Molberg poured the concrete.

People stand and wonder, "Will future anthropologists deci-
pher the imagery? Will they figure out it was built by a bass
player from Chicago who bought a shack from a woman
hunter up here in this town of only nine people?"

Take Minnesota Highway 11 west of International Falls
about 40 miles, through the towns of Loman and Indus, and
continue 8 more miles past the INDUS sign; Basshenge is on
your right, north of the highway. If you reach Birchdale you've
gone 2 miles too far. Visit Basshenge on the Web at
www.basshenge.com.

P I E   D A Y
B r a h a m

B raham claims to be the Homemade Pie Capital of Minnesota, and they've done a lot to seal that claim with their
annual Pie Day celebration. In 2001 it was held on Friday,
August 3, conflicting with the first weekend of the gigantic
Sturgis Motorcycle Rally in South Dakota; bikers who wanted
to attend both events faced a difficult compromise.

Pie Day, "beginning in the early hours of the morning and
running until dusk," featured a new event that year, the Pie
Medallion Hunt, which awarded a cash prize to whoever found
the medallion; clues were periodically revealed throughout the
day. They openly admit, in a refreshing bit of frankness, that
the purpose of the hunt was to get people to not spend all their
time at Freedom Park, where the main event is staged, and to
go snoop around the downtown.

The traditional events on Pie Day are the pie baking contest
and, following naturally, the pie eating contest (two, in fact:

junior and senior); the pie race; the art show; the small-quilt show; the artisans; and the homemade pie in the park. There is a popular booth outside the post office where they will cancel your stamps with an official Pie Day logo, and send your mail from there. There is a contest for students to solve mathematical problems with pi in them. It all builds up to 8:00 P.M., when they start the Sweety-Pie Street Dance. (An orthographer might spell that *Sweetie-Pie,* but the ladies here have been doing this for quite some time now and might not appreciate some stranger coming in with spelling advice. And, for some, it might even be the Sweaty-Pie Dance.)

Pie Day is a lot more than just the highlights: there is a pancake breakfast at the VFW Club starting at 7:00 A.M. (just like at the Sturgis Rally), an Exercise and Fitness Walk at 11:00 A.M. (unlike Sturgis), and the Pie-Alluia Chorus at the Pub & Grill on West Central Drive. They sing "songs that have to do with pies . . . or songs that have been altered to have words that have to do with pies." They had a good crowd in there at 11:45 in the morning. Throughout the day visitors visit crafters' booths and see entries in the Small Quilt Show, where quilts entered are about the size of a bath towel.

At the Pie Stage the music started at 10:00 A.M. with the St. Anthony Brass Quintet, followed by third-graders reading pie books, a bluegrass band, the WonderWeavers storytellers, the Pie-Alluia Chorus, and, at 2:00 P.M., Annie Overboe and Sue Hoss judged the pie baking. Annie and Sue are, respectively, the food editor of the *Chicago Herald* and one of the writers for *Cuisine* magazine out of Des Moines, Iowa, so they had brought in some heavy hitters, at least in the literary sense of the word.

There followed the Lumberland Cloggers and two more live music acts and at 5:30 P.M. the Junior Pie Eating Contest. The winners of the Pie A(R)t Squared Show were announced and then came the big Senior Pie Eating Contest. Only four entrants that year, compared to the maximum seven in the junior event, but the winner set a new record by eating a whole pie in one minute and forty-five seconds flat. The pies are a blueberry filling on a graham cracker crust, with whipped cream on top, "so they're easy to make and they look real good in the photograph." The pie plate ". . . doesn't have to be absolutely shiny clean, but we only allow a few crumbs left on the bottom." We asked if they furnished bibs and the woman said, "Yes. Well . . . the local mortician provides the bibs. So they're full coverage."

The prize brings fame but not riches to the winner; an old bowling trophy has been converted by removing the top and replacing it with a pie tin. The winner gets his picture and his name in the paper (or hers; women sometimes enter), and his name engraved on the pie tin, which is displayed in a store in town. It's sort of like the Stanley Cup.

Braham was named the Pie Capital of Minnesota by former governor Rudy Perpich, who was from the Iron Range; before the freeway went in the town was on the main route between the Twin Cities and Duluth and people would stop for pie at the halfway point. Fridays were the big day, with all the traffic of folks going up north to their lake cabins, so when Pie Day was begun it was natural to place it on a Friday in August.

Actually, it's a combination of two events: The Isanti County Historical Society used to hold an annual ice cream social around that same time. Ice cream and pie was a natural merger and gave rise to the famous Minnesota battle cry: "Remember the Alamode."

Braham Pie Day is held the first weekend of August. Braham is located north of Cambridge on Minnesota Highway 65 and County Road 107. Call (763) 689–4229 for information.

AS GAS STATION EXTRAORDINAIRE
Cloquet

T here is a story that Frank Lloyd Wright was once called to
testify in a court case; he took his seat on the witness stand
and an attorney asked him his name and then his occupation.
"I am the world's greatest living architect," he answered.
Chided later by his wife for his lack of modesty, he said: "I had
no choice; I was under oath."

There are two of Wright's buildings in the Cloquet area, a
house and a gas station, both owned by the same family. The
house was one of the Prairie series, built in 1954 of concrete
block, a material more closely representing the client's bank
account than the architect's preference in masonry. Making the
best of the situation, Wright had the horizontal joints, which
he called the heart lines, raked deeply back for the shadow, and
he kept the vertical joints flush with the face of the material. It
is a graceful structure, at peace with its surroundings, and the
grandson of the client still lives there.

During the budget negotiations, Wright, who wanted it done
in stone and if not that then brick, and who was famous for his
own monetary problems, asked his client: "Lindholm, don't you
know some banker you can corrupt for the money to do it?"

The R. W. Lindholm Service Station was begun in 1956, a
year that the Guggenheim Museum and eighteen other Wright
projects were under way. In 1958, during the course of the construction, his son-in-law Darrell had reason to visit him at his
office in Taliesen, in Spring Green, Wisconsin, where he asked
Wright if he might take his photo; the architect struck a
relaxed pose. The photo was printed back in Minnesota and
Darrell asked Wright's apprentice if he'd take it back and have
it signed; he came back and said the man had torn the picture
up because he looked "too old" and had sent an earlier portrait

Among architect Frank Lloyd Wright's many accomplishments:
the R. W. Lindholm Service Station in Cloquet.

back instead, signed. He was ninety years old at the time, and died the following year, proud to the end. Darrell had his negative printed again, of course, with the image of the signature on it.

The station is famous for its soaring canopy, flying optimistically unsupported out over the pumps, as well as the upstairs glass waiting lounge, built back when cars actually needed tune-ups. It is a most dramatic building and reflects Wright's enthusiasm for all things automobilian, and for the horizon; it was an integral part of his concept for the Broadacre City, as he named it, and the only component of such that was ever built.

Lindholm Service Station is found at the corner of Minnesota Highway 33 and Route 45 in Cloquet. For more information call (218) 879–2279.

THE GEEK PROM
NorShor Theater, Duluth

L et's face it: It had to happen. Once the computer began its takeover, geeks would become gods as surely as worms become butterflies. This prom was held April 13, 2002, and turned out to be a huge success in its first year. In 2003 it will only be bigger, and by 2004 it will be really cool to go to the Geek Prom. It'll be national, and people like Britney Spears and Mariano Rivera will be there, and then geeks will rule, like we know they always wanted to.

Of course no one can be turned away from a Geek Prom, no matter how cool or beautiful or how big a jock you are, because to be rejected admission to any prom at all is to become a geek right there, and then of course instantly eligible. But once inside if you don't truly let out your inner nerd and if you don't look geeky enough and act weird enough you might be shunned. And then you'll try to act cool about it but the word will get out that you went to the prom and even the geeks wouldn't have anything to do with you and . . . well, you get the drift. The other contradiction is that when it becomes way cool to go to the Geek Prom then being cool wins again, despite the triumph of the geeks.

It was organized by Paul Lundgren as a celebration of clumsy social skills and obsessive-compulsive behavior, for people who were too geeky to attend their high school prom and also for those who did go but who were too cool to properly enjoy it. They expected, and got, a "night filled with awkward romance, cheesy music and spastic fits of clumsy dancing." Paul says we're all susceptible to geekiness; he himself was jock enough to play high school football but geek enough to also be on the audiovisual squad. He told a writer of his latest geek moment, which had happened that very day as he exited his car, walked behind a pickup, saw a lovely woman, and simultaneously banged his shin on the trailer hitch. He could have acted cool but he took the Geek Choice, as he called it, and let out a loud and uncool shriek of pain.

His partner in the prom endeavor is Scott Lunt, who says a bartender named Lefty developed special geek drinks for the ball, with names like the Pocket Protector and the Leonard Nimoy. He said the Pocket Protector "actually tastes like a Pocket Protector."

The bands were Duluth's own Super D & the Double Chucks, and Vinnie and the Stardusters from Minneapolis. The former are known for their blending of 1940s country music, 1960s acid rock, and Lake Superior surf-rock into an "erratic and flamboyant three-piece nerdfest"; the latter are best known for catering to the social misfit crowd in Minneapolis with "power-rhumba parody" and "Husker Doo Doo," and for their publicity stunts. They've called the police on themselves to shut down their concerts, threatened to leave town unless a 100,000-seat stadium was built for them, and recorded an "XXXMas Song" so dirty that Howard Stern wouldn't play it. They live in the "Hub of Hell" neighborhood in Minneapolis.

A panel of Celebrity Geeks selected the King and Queen Geeks, there were limos shuttling back and forth from restaurants, they had an after-hours party (Minnesota's 1:00 A.M. closing time being geeky in itself), and they were celebrated in print and television (like CNN, dude). The prom is expected to peak in 2003; after that it could be too cool.

For more information visit www.geekprom.com; or contact Paul Lundgren (218–727–3101, manylevels@yahoo.com) or Scott Lunt (218–724–1419, starfire@duluth.com). If the Web site is not operating, try again. They are geeks, after all.

TONY'S TRADING POST
Duluth

The word *unique* has a lot of shades to it; to the folks at the Trading Post it means that you can find things here that you won't find at, say, the Mall. And that would include just about any mall, because at Tony's you can find objects to fill your special "decorating ideas for your home, office, or business." At Tony's they offer everything from weasel skulls to the mounted head of a Cape buffalo. You might need claws—perhaps lynx, badger, bear, or huge lion—and if you do, here is where to find them. They stress that everything they sell or ship is *legal,* although it may not be legal where you are from and it is your responsibility to check this out.

Need a tastefully mounted 6-foot rattlesnake? Perhaps a coyote rug or a fur cap (available from economy skunk and coonskin all the way up to jumbo lynx and timber wolf), or maybe a set of elands? It's not as bizarre as it might sound: What strikes you most when you enter the place is the sense of going back in time. It's big and it's packed with amazing things, and more convincing than a trip to a pioneer museum, even though the pioneers wouldn't have any Nazi souvenirs lying around like they do here. But they have souvenirs of all kinds of trades here, cowboys and soldiers, trappers and fishermen. And just about every creature you ever had nightmares about, from the swamp, forest, jungle, or mountain. They get these objects primarily from collections, and most have come from very good homes.

At a recent auction you could have bid on a Tibetan prayer wheel, a bronze ibex, an Australian Aborigine war ax, olivewood carvings from Israel, a handmade set of Inuit knives, a Zimbabwe medicine man mask, a monkey jug more than 2,000 years old, a silver elephant, or any of 200 other equally rare and exotic objects.

JUDY GARLAND MUSEUM

" *It's a swell state, Minnesota. We had a lovely house . . . we lived in a white house with a garden. Grand Rapids is surrounded by lakes. . . . It's a beautiful, beautiful town."* It's true that Dorothy talks about Kansas in L. Frank Baum's The Wonderful Wizard of Oz, but when Judy Garland talked about home, she talked about Grand Rapids.

Wizard was her seventh film; she was seventeen when she put her hand and shoe prints in the forecourt of Grauman's Chinese Theatre in Hollywood, an international star. She was born on June 10, 1922, in the Itasca Hospital in Grand Rapids, and christened Frances Ethel Gumm. Her father Frank owned the New Grand Theater in town; he was also a journalist and a piano player and singer who thought he would someday become a star. He was pretty much alone in this view, but his stage became the launching pad for the careers of his three daughters. The youngest, Baby Gumm, as she was called then, walked out there when she was two and a half years old and sang "Jingle Bells," and the roar of that crowd rang in her ears from then on.

They traveled northern Minnesota as a show for two years—knocking the socks off Bemidji, Cohasset, Deer Park, Hibbing, Coleraine, et al.—and they would have stayed here longer except Baby had so much talent. When she was four they took a trip to Hollywood, visited studios and got a whiff of the big time; by now they were billing themselves as Jack and Virginia Lee and the Three Little Lees, who were "fully competent to render the very latest musical numbers and the Charleston, plus black face and impersonations if desired." At three years old, Baby had done a stunning little Al Jolson routine.

They became the Gumm Sisters and made money. On a show with George Jessel in Chicago during the 1934 World's Fair, he looked down at Frances and said, "You're as pretty as a whole garland of flowers, young lady," and they instantly became the Garland Sisters. And later, as she stood ready in the wings listening to Hoagy Carmichael sing

"Judy," Frances turned to her sisters and said, "That's it! That's the name I want." The next year, at thirteen, Judy Garland signed her first movie contract with MGM.

Before she died in 1969, she would appear in thirty-two feature films; win an Oscar for Wizard of Oz; record almost a hundred singles and twenty-four albums, winning five Grammys; appear 1,100 times in concert; star in her own television show and guest on thirty others; do hundreds of radio broadcasts and military benefits; and marry five times and bear three children.

Her town hosts a world-famous Judy Jubilee here every June, where you can mingle with the Munchkins and visit the Gumm residence; and you can also walk up the Yellow Brick Road to the fabulous old Central School at 10 Northwest 5th Street, now the Itasca County Historical Society, where on the second floor you will find the largest collection of Judy Garland memorabilia in the world. And if that isn't enough there is also the Judy Garland Children's Museum at 19 Northeast 4th Street, where, among other Oz artifacts, they have the actual Emerald City Carriage, once owned by Abraham Lincoln. It's an amazing story, all of it.

The museum is located on U.S. Highway 169S and the hours are 10:00 A.M. to 5:00 P.M., seven days a week from mid-May through mid-October. Contact the Judy Garland Museum, P.O. Box 724, Grand Rapids, MN 55744. For more information call (800) 664–5839 or visit www.judygarland museum.com.

They also have a large selection of American Indian art, spirit sticks, pipes and pipe bags, fetishes, trade beads, dance costumes; they have arrowheads and longbows, and fur or leather quivers. They furnished props for the movie *Iron Will,* and Tony said, "Kevin Costner ran over one of our coyotes in *Three Thousand Miles from Graceland.*"

One person's exhilarating shopping experience of course might be another's chamber of horrors, but this is one you won't soon forget, guaranteed, whether you find something for your den or not.

Tony's Trading Post and Free Wax Museum is found at 3 West Superior Street in Duluth, or on the Web at www.tonystradingpost.com. The phone is (218) 727–3872.

WORLD OF ACCORDIONS
Duluth

It's been a remarkable journey for Helmi Harrington. She was six years old when she left Germany in 1951 with her mother, Hanni Strahl, and her grandmother. Her father had disappeared in the final weeks of World War II; they lived in Trossingen, where the Hohner accordion factory was and where her mother had trained. They had three accordions in the family, one of which had been traded for food and a second of which was thrown overboard in a random act of meanness by the ship's operator, who decided that no German immigrant needed two accordions.

Her mother accepted the sponsorship of the Second Baptist Church of Corpus Christi, Texas; did cleaning work and saved every nickel, and in a few years opened a music studio in her home. Helmi was twelve when she started giving accordion lessons there, and went on to study law and music and earn double master's degrees and a Ph.D. in musicology at the University of Texas in Austin. She then earned a Fulbright scholarship, returned to Trossingen to write her dissertation, and began a career as a concert pianist.

She came back and met Duane Sellman, a computer designer for Control Data, an advanced student in her mother's studio in Austin; they married and in 1989 moved to Minnesota. Helmi set up an accordion studio in Burnsville and then was offered the directorship of John Copisky's famous traveling Duluth Accordionaires, so they opened another studio in Duluth, in a renovated church.

It is now the largest accordion museum in the world, one of three, and one of the world's only two repair schools; students come from everywhere, ninety of them now, to study not only accordion repair and history but playing as well, on all the seven different families of the instrument.

They are of two primary types: the diatonic, wherein the instrument delivers a different tone on compression and expansion; and the chromatic, where same tone sounds in either bellows direction. With 1,000 accordions on display, there are some truly dazzling examples in the museum—from Italy, Russia, Germany, Austria, China, and the United States—done in exotic woods, inlaid with mother-of-pearl, abalone, celluloid, and rhinestones. Some of them date way back to the 1830s, nearly to the invention of the accordion and the concertina in 1829.

Helmi has become a genuine authority. She's written three books and is a lecturer, teacher, performer, and researcher, and says they will soon move into a larger place with the museum and studio. And down in Austin, Texas, her daughter Hanni Van Zandt—with the help of her brother Charles Harrington—is continuing the Strahl Music Studio as the third-generation accordion specialist.

Contact the World of Accordions Museum, 2801 West 1st Street, Duluth, MN 55806. For lessons or a tour call (218) 628–3441; or e-mail accordion@sprynet.com.

SHIP OF GHOULS

*T*he William A. Irvin *was a big ship in her day, 610 feet long and 60 feet across the beam. She (you wouldn't say "he," even if her name is William) was built in 1938 and was at the time the flagship of U.S. Steel, named after the president of the company. She had a crew of thirty-two and carried 14,000 tons of iron ore at about 11 miles an hour across the Great Lakes, powered by DeLaval cross compound steam turbines with 2,000 shaft horsepower; her forty years on the Great Lakes were called "uneventful," meaning just the usual bitterly ferocious storms and the blazing heat and all. When she retired in 1978, she had carried 1,292 loads—an average of 32 trips a year. At 11 miles an hour, you wonder how she did it.*

The flagship of the fleet also served as the hospitality center for executives; they'd come aboard in Conneaut, Ohio, and ride along for a round, wining and dining, hitting golf balls, playing cards and shuffleboard, flying kites, that sort of thing. But not fishing or swimming. Being the flagship is what saved her from the cutting torch on retirement and earned her this easy duty in port.

Her job now consists of scaring the cookies out of people in the Halloween season, and if you think an old house is scary, wait until you take this tour; the fear factor rises in direct proportion to size of the menace, and this thing is immense. The gigantic steel hull screaking and echoing in the darkness, the high catwalks and narrow passageways, the ominous piping and valves and hatches . . . in blackness, all of it would be terror on a grand scale even without any help at all from the shrieks and screams and the blood and swinging ax and the monsters and the near certainty of sudden dismemberment and all the rest of it; the gore, the eyeballs, the severed limbs—we can't go into it here, save to say it is a trip that a lot of folks are not able to finish. It is a professional-level nightmare, with help from the University of Minnesota–Duluth's Theater Department. Children under twelve aren't allowed to enjoy the experience, for their own good and for the good of their parents. Some say extra underwear for the parents is not a bad idea either.

The last entry in her log, penned by Captain John J. McDonough in 1986, reads: "She was the Queen of the Lakes and so shall she remain for the rest of her days." He had no idea it would come to this.

The William A. Irvin is moored near Duluth's Aerial Lift Bridge. To get to the ship from I–35, take Canal Park Drive, then take a right onto Railroad Street. The ship is moored at Railroad Street and Harbor Drive. For details call (218) 727–0022, ext. 234, or visit www.williamairvin.com.

AERIAL LIFT BRIDGE
Duluth

It is one of the grandest harbor entries a ship can make anywhere in the world—to traverse the entire St. Lawrence Seaway and Lakes Erie, Ontario, Huron, and Superior, then arrive with the Glensheen Mansion and downtown Duluth to starboard and a lacy steel structure as distinctive as the Eiffel Tower a mile dead ahead. You whistle the traditional "long-short, long-short" and see road traffic come to a halt and the great lift rise for your precise and majestic approach. And of course your departure is equally huge. Ships don't just sneak in and out of the Port of Duluth without anyone noticing.

The first edition wasn't even a bridge; built in 1905, the twin towers held a trestle across the top from which a gondola was hung just above the water. It traversed back and forth by a system of cables and pulleys, a suspended ferry, and carried sixty-two tons of horses, wagons, automobiles, and people. By 1929 they needed something faster and so began building the lift bridge, raising new towers right inside the old ones, lifting the fixed span 42 feet up to a clear height of 172 feet; the lift span was 386 feet long and weighed 900 tons, balanced by weights inside the towers.

They were lucky to get it built when they did. Nowadays, of course, the uncontrolled tyranny that is the highway department would simply condemn miles of the city on both ends for a long and wide approach and build a huge rising causeway, cap it in the middle with Ugly Concrete Bridge Design No. 2, and call it a job well done. But the City of Duluth owns this graceful landmark, built to fit into the city as it was and still is, and the U.S. Army Corps of Engineers owns the land around it. These are a couple of large bureaucracies not easily kicked around by the highway department, so, luckily for us, they've had to keep their clumsy mitts off.

They paint the bridge every fifteen years, which adds enough weight that they have to recalibrate the counterweights. It was given a total redo in 1986, with four new hundred-horsepower electric motors and a new operator's cabin in the center of the lift span with new radios, radar, emergency, and navigation equipment; new cables, structural repairs, and a good sand-blasting. And of course more paint.

Ships have the right-of-way over road traffic, but they have been known to wait for the passage of fire trucks; outbound ships have the right-of-way over inbound because they have less room to maneuver in the harbor. The bridge is raised an average of 5,500 times each season—the port is frozen over in winter—meaning that if you spend a summer afternoon in Duluth, you are likely to be able to watch the bridge lift and then have the giant steel side of a ship pass so close it seems you can almost, but not quite, touch it.

To view the bridge, take I–35 to Duluth and turn onto Canal Park Drive. You can't miss it.

THE CHAINSAW SISTERS SALOON
Ely

It began in 1978 when a pair of identical twins named Marlene and Michelle from the Minneapolis suburb of Richfield joined a U.S. Forest Service program for young adults. They went north to Ely and ended up working in the woods with chainsaws as part of a timber crew; to some of us it sounds like one of those programs offered as an alternative to jail time, but it wasn't that way. They liked it enough that they stayed on for

More than just a pretty name.

years, and when the Potlach Company offered some land for sale at a convergence of canoe and snowmobile trails they grabbed it up. They built a couple of cabins and thought about starting some kind of business there someday.

Eight canoe permits are issued for each day in that part of the Boundary Waters Canoe Area, and the holders would park their cars on the sisters' land while they took their canoes off on

adventures. When they came back weary and thirsty, they'd ask
if there was someplace to get a drink and suddenly things fell
into place. The Chainsaw Sisters Saloon opened in 1988 and now
attracts not only the canoe and snowmobile trade, but the locals
as well. It has become one of those You-Have-to-Go-There places.

Peak times are summer and winter, and when things are hap-
pening the place is full. People were signing the ceiling right
from the start and then began signing dollar bills and tacking
them up there; they'll come back and look for their dollar or a
friend's; Michelle says she sees "a lot of nostrils." Many bills are
from the Continent: Spain, Austria, Hungary, and so forth.

The sisters are both married; Michelle Richards runs the
saloon with her husband and Marlene Zorman works at the
Hand-Done T-Shirts Inc. operation in Ely, which of course fur-
nishes shirts for bar patrons needing a memento of the place.
Besides the shirts and the beer they have chips, pizza, sandwiches, and handmade handbags, crocheted by Michelle herself. And they have a cabin to rent, the one Marlene used to live
in. The hours vary with the season, but the place closes "when
it gets dark," which means that in winter it's shut down at 6:00
P.M. It's heated by a woodstove, and they have to haul the beer
and pop back to the house so it doesn't freeze overnight. They
have no phone and no electricity other than from their generator; the stove, refrigerator, and lights run on bottled gas.

A travel writer might say the place possesses a "unique ambience," and that would be an understatement. The ambience is
surely worth a drive through the wilderness on the Echo Trail.

From Minnesota Highway 169 east of Ely, take the Echo
Trail 6 miles north; the sign is on your right after the FENSKE
LAKE CAMPGROUND sign. Take the dirt road to Picket Lake and
the Chainsaw Sisters Saloon. For reservations call (218)
343–6840.

THE GLENSHEEN MANSION

*C*rime *is no curiosity in any state. Minnesota has had its share of attention, going back to the kidnap and murder of the Lindbergh baby, the assassination of anticrime editor Walter Liggett, attorney T. Eugene Thompson's wife's murder, the Piper kidnapping, the Brom ax murders, the disappearance of Jacob Wetterling. Many others; books have been written about St. Paul's safe haven for John Dillinger, Ma Barker, Baby Face Nelson, Machine Gun Kelly, Alvin Karpis, and Kid Cann.*

On the other end of the range of human endeavor stands the Glensheen Mansion in Duluth, a fabulously beautiful house, one of the finest in the country, now owned and maintained by the University of Minnesota. It was built by a very nice couple, Chester and Clara Congdon, both children of Methodist pastors who met at Syracuse University in New York. Chester found himself practicing law in St. Paul in 1880, five years out of college and still too poor to marry Clara; he had $9.67 in cash. But he caught a break when he met Henry Oliver of the Oliver Iron Mining Company in Duluth and became his legal counsel; U.S. Steel bought the mine in 1901 and Chester, then forty-eight, opened his own mining company. In five years he was the second richest man in Minnesota.

Clara had a degree in art and architecture and she put it to good use. The Congdons became a great asset to the city, giving it, among other things, 19 miles of Lake Superior shoreline, a landmark house, and a legacy of 7 children who have now become 300. About forty descendants still live in Duluth.

It's tough to have such a great family dragged into sensational headlines by one person, but the youngest daughter of Chester and Clara, the kindhearted Elisabeth—who had never married, staying home to care for the parents—had adopted two girls. One of these was Marjorie, whose second husband was Roger Caldwell. In 1977, when Elisabeth was eighty-three, the Caldwells came to Duluth to ask for an $800,000 advance on her inheritance and were refused. Shortly afterward Elisabeth and her nurse were found murdered in the mansion. The whole nation heard about it.

Marjorie and Roger were tried separately and things got confused and in the end both were freed. She remarried while still married to Roger, and then her new husband and his ex-wife both died of suspicious causes; the details of it all are far too dreary for a book of curiosities, save to say that Roger committed suicide and Marjorie now lives in Arizona. Lives in a prison there. Finally. Locked up for arson when sheriff's deputies caught her in the act. By coincidence, a long string of fires in her and her neighbors' properties immediately ended.

But the Glensheen Mansion in Duluth is a sweet place to visit; 85,000 people do so every year, and they go home and tell their friends about it. It is so magnificent as to make folks forget about crime for a while.

The Glensheen Mansion is located 5 miles northeast of downtown Duluth on Minnesota Highway 61 at 3300 London Road. The mansion is open extended summer hours. November through April it is open Friday through Sunday only, 11:00 A.M. to 2:00 P.M. For tour information call (218) 726–8910 or (888) 454–GLEN or visit www.d.edu.umn/glen.

LIFE 60 BELOW
Embarrass

The mean annual temperature here is 34.4 degrees, a full degree colder than anyplace else in the state. In 1996 they had a stretch of twenty-five straight days below zero; a plaque at the Timber Hall in Embarrass states that on February 2, 1996, the temperature reached sixty-four below, Fahrenheit. It had been an exciting day because the official electronic thermometer had quit at fifty-three below—a power failure caused by all the television crews—and nearby Tower hit an official sixty below, a new record. Men were pounding nails into wood boards with bananas, just for the sport.

There was a party of weather masochists up from the Twin Cities who slept under the snow outside the Timber Hall that night and had four thermometers with them, all reading sixty-two to sixty-four below. A Taylor recorded the minus sixty-four degrees and was sent to a testing laboratory, where it was certified dead accurate. So the record isn't a National Weather Service record, but it's the real record.

Embarrass is more a township than a town; no church, no bar, and you can't drive around the block there. It's stretched along County Road 21 between Minnesota Highway 135 and County Road 362. The town hall is at Salo Corner, along with the Corner Cafe and the visitor center, and the post office is a couple of miles east, near the gas station, the bottle shop, and the Timber Hall (incidentally, the nation's second largest freestanding log structure), and there isn't that much in between them. The 814 residents live scattered through the adjacent timberland and open country; it sits in a beautiful valley on the Laurentian Divide, between two rivers flowing in opposite directions. The Pike flows north to Lake Vermilion and the Rainy River, the Embarrass south to the St. Louis River and Lake Superior.

The French named it the Rivières des Embarras, meaning "river with barriers or obstructions," because of frequent log-jams in spring. It has nothing to do with being embarrassed about cold weather, and in fact the residents are proud of getting themselves regular national bylines. People have moved here from Arizona, Alabama, and the Marshall Islands, just for the cold.

Roland Fowler is the township foreman/coordinator and longtime community leader—a veteran, one of the last of the army's mule skinners—and also the keeper of the weather station at Embarrass, which means he's been on national television. He talks slowly and directly. "There's no way the Falls can keep up with us," he says about International Falls, the so-called Icebox of the Nation. "Even in July we have had the lowest temperatures. We have had overnight killing frosts in July." Asked in an interview how cold it was in Embarrass—it was between fifty and sixty below at the time—he said: "Well, let me put it this way . . . we don't have a lot of dope dealers hanging out on the corners today."

Embarrass is located east on CR 21 off MN 135 between Tower and Virginia. Town tours are conducted daily at 10:00 A.M. and 2:00 P.M. from Memorial Day through Labor Day. Contact the Town of Embarrass, P.O. Box 118, 7503 Levander Road, Embarrass, MN 55732. For more information call (218) 984-2084 or visit www.embarrass.com.

THE CABIN OF THE ROOT BEER LADY

*H*er name was Dorothy Molter, born in 1907 in Arnold,
Pennsylvania, one of six children of Mattie and Cap
Molter. Mattie died when Dorothy was seven; the children
found themselves in an orphanage in Cincinnati until Cap
remarried, moved to Chicago, and brought them all back
together.

She graduated from the Chicago Nursing School in 1930,
just in time for the Great Depression. With employment
opportunities slim, she went fishing with her father and
stepmother that summer at a small resort on Knife Lake
near the Canadian border: four rough cabins on three
islands called the Isle of Pines, connected by log bridges and
all built by a retired logger named Bill Berglund. He needed
someone to help run the camp. She figured it beat waiting
by a phone in Chicago, and moved to the resort. "It was a
real adventure for a young woman," she said in 1980. "I've
been here ever since and I have no intention of leaving."

Bill died in 1948 and left the islands to her, and she
returned to Chicago only enough to keep her nurse's certifi-
cate current. In winter she lived in a cabin on the largest
island, and in summer she'd move into the tent cabin and
rent the other four out. She made good root beer and sold it
to campers, hikers, fishermen, and snowmobilers. There were
about 6,000 to 7,000 visitors a year, for whom she made
11,000 to 12,000 bottles of root beer; a remarkable accom-
plishment for a lone person 15 miles from the nearest road.
In 1952 the Saturday Evening Post ran an article about her,
billing her as "the Loneliest Woman in America." She would
later say that even though in midwinter she yearned for
summer and in midsummer she missed the quiet times, "I've
never been lonely in my life . . . I have an extensive library of
books to read. I snowshoe over the frozen lakes and through
the forest each day for several miles. I fish through the ice

and shoot partridge and other game birds for food. My animal friends visit me every day. I cut wood from fallen trees and carry the logs back on a sled pulled by my snowmobile. I don't have time to get lonely."

She died in her cabin in 1986, at age seventy-nine, after living fifty-six years in what became the Boundary Waters Canoe Area, a million acres, the largest wilderness preserve east of the Rockies. Two of the cabins were moved to Ely, log by log, to become a museum; it took fifty-seven air flights, plus an uncounted number of dogsled and snowmobile runs, to bring the logs and furniture out. A brewery is now making a Dorothy Molter Root Beer from her recipe, with part of the proceeds going to maintain the museum.

In her last years she was the only permanent resident in the BWCA; everyone else had died or been evicted and every structure, including her rental cabins, had been bought by the U.S. government. Impossible to imagine what it would be like to be the only resident in a million acres of forest. She wasn't even allowed to sell her root beer, but if you stopped by in your canoe she'd give you one, and you were allowed to put something in the donation jar.

The Dorothy Molter Museum is open 10:00 A.M. to 6:00 P.M. seven days a week from Memorial Day until September. It is located at 2002 Sheridan Street in Ely. Call (218) 365–4451 for information.

HOCKEY HALL OF FAME
Eveleth

The town calls itself the Hockey Capital of the United States. A certain country to the north has a Hockey Hall of Fame in Toronto, but Eveleth has their own Hall of Fame, with a Great Hall featuring the 1960 and 1980 Olympic gold medal teams. They claim that no other town of their size has done more for the sport in this country than Eveleth. And in fact four of their players were on the 1956 U.S. Olympic team and two local players, John Mariucci and John Brimseth, are enshrined in the Toronto version.

But of course what gets them into this book is yet another outlandishly overdone sculpture, this one the World's Largest Hockey Stick. And it's huge, 107 feet long, which is about twice as long as the Jolly Green Giant is tall. It was laminated at the Christian Brothers factory down the road in Warroad and hauled over on a traffic-stopping big rig in 1995; it's mounted as if about to slap a 700-pound hockey puck across the street at the big goalie mural over there. And as over-the-top as it all sounds, it's actually pretty doggone tasteful. The wood is beautiful and the whole thing is more art than road cheese. In fact, we'd just flat say that it's art. We take back the part about outlandish. It's pretty cool.

The U.S. Hockey Hall of Fame is at 801 Hat Trick Avenue in Eveleth. Phone (800) 443–7825 or (218) 744–5167.

POLKA MASS

On May 5, 1973, in the Resurrection Catholic Church of Eveleth, Minnesota, Father Frank Perkovich held the first Polka Mass known to the modern world. He took to heart the freeing spirit of Vatican II and had hymns adapted to traditional Slovenian and Croatian folk music, as performed by Joe Cvek and the Variables and a men's singing group, the Choraleers.

In 1975 a Chicago newspaper reporter wrote about the Polka Mass and the national wire services picked up on the story, leading to the good father's performing at churches and festivals around the world, and ultimately to an invitation in 1983 from the pope himself to do a Polka Mass at the Vatican. Quite the deal for a humble working polka band to play under the high painted domes and arches of the fabulous ancient Basilica of St. Peter.

When Father Perk, as he's known to his parishioners, moved to St. Joseph's Catholic Church in Gilbert in 1987, he brought his polka tradition with him. The musicians are now called Joe Cvek and the Polka Massters—the singers are now the Perkatones—and the Mass is performed only on special occasions such as the Fourth of July and Labor Day weekends. Father Perk is now seventy; he was inducted into the Ironwood USA Polka Hall of Fame in 1991 and into the Cleveland Style Polka Hall of Fame in 1992.

But the priest and the Polka Massters do keep up a schedule of guest appearances, and if you go they'd just as soon that you leave your dancing shoes at home. The idea has spread some, and certain of the imitators get a little wild; Father Perk prefers Mass without fancy costumes and without drums. He told a magazine writer: "There have been some variations. Some, to my regret, have too much oompah-pah."

To contact Father Perk for future schedules, his Web site is www.rangenet.com/~fr-perk/index.html.

NANIBOUJOU LODGE
Grand Marais

In 1928 Babe Ruth, Jack Dempsey, Ring Lardner, and a circle of lesser notables got together and built a fabulous lodge on the beautiful North Shore of Lake Superior—easy to sling the superlatives around when you're talking about this place—which is operating to this day, offering great rooms and wonderful meals, all at reasonable prices. And for a little extra you can even get a room with a fireplace, but you won't get one with a telephone or a television. You are supposed to get away from all that up here.

The food is good enough to write a 125-page book about and they have, titled *Dining in the Spirit of Naniboujou,* with full-color photos of the lodge and eighty succulent recipes. It would be near understatement to call the high-ceilinged main dining room "stunning," richly decorated as it is in Cree Indian motifs, hung with intricate paper chandeliers, and containing the largest native stone fireplace in the state. Two hundred tons, that fireplace weighs.

The lodge is on the National Register of Historic Places and is located near the Gunflint Trail, the Boundary Waters Canoe Area, and the Superior National Forest. We can't think of anything else you'd need. Certainly not a television.

They are located at 20 Naniboujou Trail; the mailing address of the Naniboujou Lodge and Restaurant is HC-1, Box 505, Grand Marais 55604. The phone number is (218) 387–2688.

Aubin Photo Shop
Hibbing

Paul Aubin's father dropped out of high school in Ely in the mid-1890s and came to Hibbing to work in a photo studio; he started his own shop in 1907, when he was in his early twenties. When Paul was nine years old his father built him a darkroom in the basement and paid him a half penny apiece to make black-and-white jumbo enlargements, so he always had "spending money for ice cream at the grocery store."

A time, a place, a way of life—in 14,000 images.

His father ran the place until he was eighty-seven years old
and in the process collected more than 400 cameras, including
the first model Kodak 16mm movie camera ever made, one of
only a few still around. There is a rare pre–World War II Japanese military aerial camera with a motor wind and metal
crosshairs for a viewfinder, heavy as a good-sized anvil; Paul
has no idea how the old man acquired it.

The hundreds of cameras on display are worth a visit to the
place, but beyond the remarkable hardware is the print collection, over 14,000 images on file, chronicling the history of a
city that packed up and moved down the road; a mining industry that made it possible for us to win World War II; and thousands of weddings, proms, and family histories, from an age
and a people unique in American history. The store has become
almost a museum-in-waiting since Wal-Mart moved to town and
took about 80 percent of their film and finishing business; Paul
is seventy-four and various historical societies have asked him
for the contents of the place. The best time to see it is now,
while it's still in its own sweet building and is a functioning
business. It's a vanishing species, the small shop and studio,
and you won't find one like this one anywhere.

Contact Aubin Photo Service, 1801 3rd Avenue East, Hibbing
55746; (218) 263–7772.

GREYHOUND BUS MUSEUM
Hibbing

The bus industry began right up there on the Iron Range,
the direct result of one man's shortcomings as a salesman;
its story is told in the angular red, white, and blue bus
museum, brought into existence by another man's enthusiasm
and persistence.

*In 1914 Carl Erick Wickman quit his day job and began
America's bus industry—carting Hibbing's miners to and from
their jobs for fifteen cents a ride.*

In the spring of 1914, a Swedish immigrant named Carl
Erick Wickman got tired of being an iron miner—hard to
believe, but true—and he put his savings into a Hupmobile
agency; he had one car to sell. A lot of miners wanted to ride
and test drives would usually end up at the Hull-Rust Mine,
but miners weren't really the Hupmobile's natural clientele.
Carl got frustrated after a few months and started charging fifteen cents for a ride.

A good part of Hibbing sat directly over iron ore deposits;
buildings in the direct path of progress were put on rollers and
moved south to a settlement called Alice. Over time, a substan-
tial part of the town had been carted off and was sitting 2 miles
down the road; a test ride in the Hupmobile down to Alice

would save forty minutes of walking, and the car was full almost from the minute it went into operation. They offered a round trip for twenty-five cents and were making ten bucks a day right from the get-go.

It quickly wasn't big enough and Wickman's partner, ex-miner Andrew Anderson—who became known as Bus Anderson—took a cutting torch to the frame, welded in an extension, and installed more seats; the weight of the extra passengers put the fenders right down on the tires and it wouldn't budge. Stiffer springs cured that, and the flame of Anderson's torch had lit two American core industries, the bus line and the stretch limo.

Fifteen people would be riding at once, hanging all over the thing. They recruited partners and stretched their cars and soon had a line to Nashwauk, and they became the Hibbing Transportation Company, dubbed the Snoose Line by the tobacco-chewing riders. In December 1915 they grew into the Mesabi Transportation Company and in a few months had eighteen vehicles on the road. They hooked up with the Great Northern Railroad and by 1925 had 150 buses. Headquarters moved to Chicago and the name changed to Greyhound; today it's in Dallas and 19 million annual passengers take 18,000 daily departures to 2,600 destinations. And not one of them is named Hibbing, Minnesota.

Sometime around 1974, in Hibbing's sadly abandoned bus depot, a grocer named Gene Nicolleli found a dusty old sign that read BIRTHPLACE OF THE BUS INDUSTRY IN THE UNITED STATES. He did some research and found a remarkable story, and he thought someone should build a museum in his town and he should be that person. He lobbied governors and legislators for fifteen years for backing and finally in 1989 a small museum opened. In 1999 the dynamic new building was finished; it holds seven historically significant buses and a ton of surprising bus paraphernalia. Another of those things you take for granted that turn out to be far more interesting than you thought they would.

To get to the Greyhound Bus Origin Center, take 13th Street off U.S. Highway 169 going northeast out of Hibbing. The center is open mid-May through September from 9:00 A.M. to 5:00 P.M. and Sunday 1:00 P.M. to 5:00 P.M. For more information write to 1201 East Greyhound Boulevard, Hibbing 55746; call (218) 263–5814 or (218) 263–6485; or visit www.greyhoundbus museum.com.

WORLD'S LARGEST PIT
Hibbing

The Hull-Rust-Mahoning Mine is called the Grand Canyon of the North, a misnomer given it by an enthusiast at the chamber of commerce who believed it was dug by employees of the state tourism board to attract Iowans to northeastern Minnesota. The unpainted truth is that it was dug by great gangs of mercenaries, some of them foreign nationals from Finland and Italy; their descendants still populate the Iron Range, three generations later, and are proud to be called Rangers. They don't move into other parts of Minnesota, because life is too soft in those places.

Iron mining is cleaner than coal mining but it's similar in that the miners don't have to be searched at the end of a shift, the way they do in gold and diamond mines. You couldn't carry a dollar's worth of iron ore away in a wheelbarrow and even if you could you'd have a hard time selling it on the street. And pawnshops won't touch iron ore.

It is the world's largest open ore pit, 3 miles long, 1½ miles wide, and 600 feet deep. From it has come some 30 percent of the nation's iron ore in the last century, more than 800,000,000 tons of it. The mines are quiet now, but when blasting used to shake the town of Hibbing three times a day, nobody ever minded; it sounded to them like the rumble of money. There were more than fifty mining companies here at one time, some open pit and some vertical shaft, and as the endeavor grew most of them merged into this one large canyon, today filled 300 feet deep with spring-fed water and looking like a pristine mountain lake. They had to move 1.4 billion tons of earth to get at all that ore; each bucketful of the loader held 33 cubic yards, more than three large ready-mix cement trucks can carry, and their 240-ton trucks—nine times the capacity of the average highway semi trucks—have engines with sixteen cylinders, four turbochargers, and 1,600 horsepower. Tires tall as a basketball rim.

Hibbing itself is unusual in that it used to sit right over what is now the pit. Only a few streets and some foundations remain along the edge from 1919, when they had to move off the iron; it's now a town of 17,071 people sitting a couple of miles away. It was like moving the dog off the couch.

To reach the Hull-Rust-Mahoning Mine, follow signs from U.S. Highway 169 through a residential neighborhood in north Hibbing. The mine is open to the public 9:00 A.M. to 7:00 P.M. daily year-round, with free admission. Call the Iron Trail Convention & Visitors Bureau at (218) 262–4900 or (800) 777–8497 or visit www.irontrail.org for more information.

MAILBOAT
Lake Vermilion

Lake Vermilion would be on the Top Three Lakes list of almost everyone in Minnesota for its beauty, its size, the water, the perfect campsites, and the amazing tranquillity of its bays. It's a lake with 365 islands, so you could visit a different one every day of the year. It is also the locale of one of only two water mail routes in the state, the other being a mailboat that circles Isle Royale in Lake Superior and makes fewer than ten stops.

The mailboat on Vermilion covers 110 miles and delivers to some fifty to seventy-five island cabins, leaving its dock at the Aronson Boat Works six days a week at 9:00 A.M. and returning sometime after 1:00 P.M.; the 21-foot Lund boat will take up to six passengers for a fee, and they recommend that you call ahead for reservations. The season runs from the first of June through the first week in September.

The pilots, who double as tour guides, change every year or two, but they maintain a tradition that goes back to 1923, when John Aronson's father contracted with the Postal Service to deliver mail. In those days the boat was bigger and was mainly a water taxi, delivering everything from groceries to construction materials; most of the older cabins here were built with lumber delivered by mailboat.

It's a different world up there. Dogs come out to the end of the dock to greet the mailman, tails wagging, running around, excited to see him; the mailman's different, too, because he carries two pouches of mail and a pouch of dog biscuits. A pooch pouch. They go through five pounds of dog biscuits a month, donated by a couple of longtime lake families. If there's no mail for an address the carrier will pull in there anyway and flip the dog a biscuit; in one stretch there are three mailbox docks in a row and a pair of dogs run out to the end of each of them and score each time, figuring they've got the guy fooled into thinking there are six dogs.

The arrival of the mailman is a big deal to people, too; a lot of folks don't even have a television set, by preference, and to many he's the only daily contact with the outside world. He's got a cell phone for emergencies, so if you're going to have one it's best to try to hold off until just before the mailboat arrives.

Call the Aronson Boat Works in Tower at (218) 753–4190 for information.

THE HINCKLEY FIRE MUSEUM

*I*n 1860 eastern Minnesota and western Wisconsin were covered by a vast forest. When it was opened to logging they found white pines 120 feet tall; logging towns sprang up throughout the forest, and Hinckley sawmills kept two rail lines busy to St. Paul. In the drought years of the early 1890s, fires in the underbrush and slash were so common the sky rarely cleared.

September 1, 1894, was blazing hot and dry; outlying fires and a breeze brought smoke so thick that payroll clerks lit lanterns to see their work. A wind whipped up about 1:00 P.M. and a telegraph came from Pokegama, to the south, saying the town was burning furiously and could not be saved. The gray smoke in Hinckley turned suddenly black; the local priest set out running through the streets, shouting for all to get out of the path of the fire.

It didn't take much urging. People ran to the Grindstone River and some ran out to the gravel pit; seventy-five ran to the Eastern Minnesota Railroad station where two trains sat, a passenger and a freight, waiting to leave. The engineers coupled the two together and people piled into empty boxcars. They cleared the trestle south of town as the timbers burned beneath them and paint blistered on the cars. The depot agent sent out a telegraph warning to the next station in Barnum, adding "I think I've stayed too long" as fire took the depot.

To the north of town people found barely 3 inches of water in the river and gravel pit; they headed up the tracks and met a crowded southbound St. Paul & Duluth passenger train under the throttle of Jim Root. He braked and a hundred people crammed on board. As he backed up, the forest erupted in flames. The first water would be Skunk Lake, 6 miles up; the worst 6 miles any engineer ever held a throttle to. Winds were whipping the fire around them so hard the glass blew out of the cab, set the curtain on fire, set the very coal in the tender behind them on fire. When they finally reached the lake they dragged Root out of the cab; he left the skin and the meat of his right hand sizzling on the throttle. His shirt was burned, he was blistered and unconscious and not expected to live.

The other train made Sandstone, 8 miles to the south and stopped briefly, but they'd heard so many fire warnings there that not one person would get on; they wouldn't even put their children aboard. Twenty minutes later fire leveled the village.

The smoke could be seen in central Wisconsin and in Iowa. In all, 418 people perished and six towns burned. Thirty miles north and twenty-four years later it happened again, in Moose Lake, when 450 died in a fire that nearly reached Duluth.

Hinckley Fire Museum is located at 106 Old Highway 61. Take the Hinckley exit off I–35N then west on County Road 48 to Old Highway 61 and turn right. The museum is open May 1 through mid-October, Tuesday through Saturday from 10:00 A.M. to 5:00 P.M. Closed Monday. For information call (800) 996–4566 or (320) 384–0126 or visit www.hinckleymn.com/heritage.html.

NEUTRINOS
Soudan Mine

You wouldn't think that a fun family outing in a creaky cage dropping you half a mile down into the deepest mineshaft in Minnesota would put you face to face with stuff like neutrinos, muons, wimps, taus, proton decay, and quantum physics, but there they are. There are scientists down there to measure neutrinos to be sent up from Batavia, Illinois, near Chicago; sent straight through the ground, so as to avoid the Illinois Tollway. Doing basic research, to determine things like the ultimate fate of the universe. (Expanding Forever? . . . Or Heading for the Big Crunch? . . . The answer when we come back from a break. . . .)

We know all about this stuff, no problem, but when you're on a mine trip and you run into dark matter—matter even darker than the walls of the shaft—it's best not to go into explanations. A time like that is a time to relax and enjoy your neutrinos. Take 'em as they come, and don't worry about the end of the universe. It'll be here soon enough, and no point hurrying it along, either.

Iron ore was discovered on the Vermilion Range at Soudan during the Minnesota Gold Rush of 1865—sounds like a joke, doesn't it?—but they didn't start mining it until 1882, waiting for technology to catch up with them. The first ore was shipped from the Soudan Mine to Two Harbors on July 31, 1884, which was the very first day of the Iron Range. Seems odd; we've assumed it was always called the Iron Range, even before they found iron there; that maybe even the Indians called it that.

They brought 15.5 million tons of iron ore up this narrow shaft, this one and the Alaska shaft, before they ceased operations in 1962. U.S. Steel donated the mine and 1,300 acres to the state as a park in 1965; it's visited annually by 39,298 people and by some 24,000 bats. The bats don't go down to the lowest level; they kind of stay out of the way somewhere up near the entrance. There are twenty-seven levels and 50 horizontal miles of mine tunnels down there, and they take you down 2,341 feet to the bottom. There is a new mural there in the big main room, a brilliant portrait of the sun, and it's not only beautiful but also the world's deepest mural.

The temperature in the mine is fifty degrees year-round, except inside the Cryogenic Dark Matter Search detector, where it's minus 459.69—a slim hundredth of a degree above Absolute Zero. Which makes it colder than Embarrass by 396 degrees, and the coldest place in Minnesota.

The town of Soudan is located on Minnesota Highway 169 between Virginia and Ely. The Soudan Underground Mine State Park conducts underground tours seven days a week on the hour, 10:00 A.M. to 4:00 P.M. There is a tour fee. Bring warm clothing. For information call (218) 753–2245, e-mail soudan-mine@dnr.state.mn.us, or visit www.dnr.state.mn.us/state_parks/soudan_underground_mine/index.html.

You Can Lead a Bear to Doughnuts, but You Don't Really Need To

*T*here are about 30,000 black bears in Minnesota, mostly in the north, and it only takes one three-thousandth of 1 percent of the bear population—one—to break into your cabin, eat all your food, and trash the place. They aren't mean by nature but they'll eat anything and they generally weigh between 250 and 500 pounds, and they can run 35 miles an hour and they have pitchfork claws and ice-tong teeth and a truck-tire hide, and they can climb trees.

Vince Shute grew up as a logger on his grandfather's homestead, moved to a nearby spot in the woods in 1944, and pretty much stayed put from then on. He ran a logging company, meaning he had to pay and feed and look out for a big crew of loggers. When he'd leave his shack for any length of time, he'd sometimes come back to find the subtle signs of bear: the smashed-in front door, the broken-down empty cupboards, the busted furniture, and the total absence of edibles. He'd take his rifle and find the culprit, who would not be offered much in the way of due process; certainly not bail or parole.

But Vince was a big guy and he wasn't mean by nature either, any more than the bears were, and he concluded they weren't wrecking his place out of malice but just from hunger, something he himself had grown up with, so he began to set out leftovers from the T. Patton Cafe in Orr as protection money. And he had a legendary rapport with animals—so much so that a friend of his said when he was growing up their family dog would run around and bark and wag his tail about ten minutes before Vince dropped in; he could feel his presence out there. He said, "Vince was the most thoroughly good person I've ever met, and animals can sense that."

The bears not only quit trashing the shack, they brought in relatives and they all became Vince's pals. He gave them names and they started a syndicate, with a few of them getting very large, especially Duffy, who hit 816 pounds and became the world's largest black bear; the Don Corleone of Minnesota, who would share giant Patton doughnuts with Vince and keep lesser bears in line.

Before Vince passed on he realized that without him his bears would become vulnerable to hunters, so in 1995 his friends formed the ABA, the American Bear Association (the more famous ABA is known as an association of sharks), taking his 40 acres and adding 320 more and creating the Vince Shute Wildlife Sanctuary. They built a viewing platform that is now the best place in North America to view black bears in their natural habitat.

The Vince Shute Wildlife Refuge is 1 mile south of Orr on U.S. Highway 53. Turn left onto County Road 23 and continue on for 13 miles, just past County Road 514. It's on your right. The sanctuary is open Memorial Day through Labor Day, 5:00 P.M. until dusk, Monday through Saturday. Closed Sunday. Contact the American Bear Association, P.O. Box 77, Orr 55771; call (800) 357–9255; or e-mail bears@ rangenet.com.

TWIN CITIES

TWIN CITIES

MALL OF AMERICA
Bloomington

Here's a collection of miscellaneous superlatives: Seven Yankee Stadiums would fit inside its volume; it was built using 13,300 short tons of steel, twice as much as in the Eiffel Tower in Paris; it holds 4 major department stores, 525 specialty shops, 50 restaurants, 7 nightclubs, and 14 movie theaters; and it draws 42 million people a year, nine times the population of the whole state and more than Disney World, Yellowstone Park, and the Grand Canyon put together.

It has a most direct parking ramp, which makes the experience much easier than you would expect—you drive straight up the ramp and straight down the other side; pick your floor as you see it. No spirals. It sits on the old Metropolitan Stadium ground, former home of the Twins and Vikings. Home plate is marked in Camp Snoopy, the entertainment park in the center, which also has 30,000 plants and 400 live trees. On a good day there are twice as many people in the Mall as there are in the entire city of Bloomington, where it sits; the state's third largest city, with 90,000 residents.

When it was opened in August 1992 the experts said the market was saturated and the megamall combination would never work. A Chicago wizard was quoted: "The whole project flies in the face of this high-stressed, need-focused consumer of today. . . . Entertainment and retailing, it will not work. They are in direct conflict with one another. They couldn't have designed it worse in terms of creating a consumer nightmare." As one ages, one begins to realize that folks who make statements like this are seldom taken to task ten years later when they are proven dead wrong. A person can pretty much get everything backward and still get away with it; this is perhaps useful information to pass on to one's grandchildren.

Anyway, more than 1,500 couples have been married here, an average of 3 a week. Hard to say if that proves anything.

To get to the Mall of America, take Interstate 494, then exit at Minnesota Highway 77 or 24th Avenue; head south to 81st Street or Killibrew Drive. You won't miss it.

COFFEEPOT WATER TOWER
Lindstrom: "America's Little Sweden"

Well, the big thing about it is that steam comes out of the spout. You see the classic tower with that coffeepot up there with the welcome on it, and it looks good; but if you happen to look up and catch it when the steam is on, it's really quite the deal.

It's not their real water tower anymore, not since they got the new one in 1992, but a couple of community-minded citizens stepped forward to keep the old 1908 version standing and to turn it into a Swedish symbol, because of local cultural ties to the old country, and of course the coffeepot would be the ultimate Swedish symbol. A company was hired to take the ladder off, build an access door, add the button on the top, the handle, and the spout; and then to paint it white with the hand-lettered VELKOMMEN TILL LINDSTROM, and the Swedish rosemaling on the two sides.

It all went over so well that a city employee got to work on the idea of having steam come out of the spout, using the fire department's practice smoke generator, the same type of gear used for smoke at rock concerts. In 1994 they rigged the piping to get the smoke up to the spout so they could have fifteen minutes of steam four times a day, although they only fire it up during the summer months. There are lights at the base to highlight the coffeepot at night.

They are quick to point out that not a bit of the expense for any of this came from tax dollars. This is private enterprise at work here, and private charity in the best sense of the word. It is definitely not a case of public-funded frivolity, and please bear that in mind when you see it.

The water tower is located on the main street of Lindstrom. Watch for the steam. Call the City of Lindstrom at (651) 257–0620 for information on times.

K-9 CAFE
Minneapolis

There is a shop in Minneapolis called the Mel-O-Glaze Bakery and Donut Shop, operated by the Bosela family since 1961. It has been a neighborhood institution for most of its existence and has recently turned a portion of its floor space over to the serving of all-natural treats for dogs; treats such as the Party On banana cakes shaped like bones, heart-shaped carob cakes covered with Cool Whip, the You'd Better Take Me Seriously Poodle Puffs with whipped topping, and the Doberman doughnuts. From a purely aesthetic standpoint, the dog pastries are far prettier than the people pastries.

Folks bring their dogs in and they sit around small tables and have coffee and sweet rolls while the dogs eat the more

*A regular customer points out his preference at a display of
delicate pastries.*

beautiful healthier all-natural treats out of dishes on the floor;
stuff made from whole wheat and soy flour, sunflower and
pumpkin seeds, molasses, spinach, carrots. All the wholesome
foods dogs ate before they were domesticated and given plain
old Puppy Chow. It can get to be a busy place at times but even
then it's not as noisy as one might expect. A certain dog protocol kicks in and they maintain their social graces, keeping in
check whatever natural secret urges they might have.

They have birthday parties, of course, and slices of cake are passed around not only to the invited dog guests but also to whomever dogs might be there at the time. People seem to enjoy the atmosphere and the chance to bring their pets to a place where they can all eat together. If the idea catches on, one might expect it to go in the direction of bring-your-dog hamburger joints, and from there into upscale canine steak houses. It would beg the question: Would PETA picket a place where dogs eat meat?

The K-9 Cafe is at 28th Avenue and Minnehaha Parkway in Minneapolis. It's open 9:00 A.M. to 9:00 P.M. Wednesday through Sunday. Call (612) 729–7300.

NYE'S POLONAISE
Minneapolis

For some of us, this place has everything. It has a real history, it's posh, it's funky, the food is great, the prices are reasonable, the service is good, and there's live music both in the bar and the dining room.

The building on the corner of Hennepin and Prince was built in the 1880s and for years was a workingman's bar named Hefron's; Al Nye bought it in 1950 and kept it close to its roots. He was a machine shop foreman himself and he knew his crowd and he did well at hosting them, well enough that in 1964 he was able to acquire the place next door for a dining addition, which he named the Polonaise Room. It's all still there just as he designed it: curved piano bar with a Chopin portrait hanging above it, red carpeting, dark wood paneling, gold-flecked overstuffed booths. The specialties are prime rib, lobster, and Polish food, including Al's own recipes for cabbage rolls, sausage, and short ribs.

The World's Most Dangerous Polka Band.

All of which went over so well that in a few years he annexed the next building in the block, a former harness shop listed on the National Register of Historic Places, which became the Chopin Dining Room; and in 1974 he added the diner next door, Jon's Cafe, into the mix. Redecorated the place and hung pictures of military officers and called it the Pulaski Room, after the Polish-born general who helped us win the Revolutionary War.

It isn't just the food and the ambience that brings the crowds; in the original corner bar, unchanged in fifty years, there is a tiny stage between the cigarette machine and the men's room with a worn dance floor in front of it, and pressed onto the stage are the Ruth Adams Band, who call themselves the World's Most Dangerous Polka Band but whom the bartender smilingly calls the Wax Museum Trio. Ruth plays accordion and is rumored to know a couple thousand songs, the horn players change from week to week, and Al Ophus sits behind a small drum kit slathered in autographs; he sings, tells jokes, and looks younger than his rumored eighty-seven years. They played on national television in 1995 from New York and were a big hit.

In the more elegant Polonaise Room another veteran entertainer holds forth. Lou Snider's been at the piano bar for thirty years, from well before karaoke, and she can cover whatever tunes the Dangerous Polka Band doesn't. She's dealt with a lot of situations there and still enjoys the scene, and still makes folks feel good; lately both she and the band have become popular among the twenties set. Employees say the average age in the bar has dropped from fifty to thirty in the last five years.

The bartender says, ". . . It's like working at a resort up north; people just come here to have fun. Nobody cares how you dress, how good can you sing, none of that. It's all just fun."

Nye's is at 112 East Hennepin in Minneapolis. The Ruth Adams Band plays Thursday through Saturday nights. Call (612) 379–2021 for information.

THE GUM LADY

*V*aleri Boettcher is the world's undisputed champion gum collector, listed in the 2000 edition of the Guinness Book of World Records as having 2,646 different unopened packages; her fame has grown and people have since sent her 886 more. So now it's 3,532.

She's become more than a collector these days; she can tell you the various ways gum is made and its history all the way back to the mastica tree in Greece in the year 50; a number so low it looks like a misprint. Her own gum history dates back to when she was fourteen years old and she collected 250 Bazooka wrappers, which she sent in for a Fonzie necklace—the guy in Happy Days—and suddenly packets of gum became interesting to her. Twenty-four years later she's world champ.

She has exotic gums from France, Japan, Denmark, Tahiti, Zimbabwe, Germany, Korea; garlic-flavored gum from Italy. She has gum made in 1918, a 1932 Wrigley's Juicy Fruit, and a rare 1947 Warrens Mint Cocktail. A 2-foot by 3-foot Chiclets box from Mexico hangs from the light fixture in her dining room. There is gum in the shape of guitars, of brains and lips; gum with names like Chimp Ears and Uncle Sillie's Food Fight. And of course all that gum with sports cards, movie cards, and television cards.

When she first told her husband-to-be about the collection, he said "You have what?" But he's since become a big help; he encouraged her to go public in 1994, telling her if she didn't someday all those trunks full of packets would be lost. And there are a lot of trunks; the basement of their house is nearly full. She is thinking these days of a gum museum, with a room for history and another to show the manufacturing process; and of course a really big room to show off the collection.

She says some 550 companies make gum, 60 of them in Turkey. The United States, England, and Canada are next, and other makers are scattered throughout the world. She has samples from most of them. But what she doesn't have is the very model that started it all: the Jumbo Bazooka, which was made in three or four flavors. She's also missing five flavors of Bubs Daddy. If anyone out there can help, please contact her: Valerie Boettcher, 13310 North 40th Street, Baytown Township, MN 55082.

An awful lot of gum for one woman—especially one who chews it only when pressured by photographers.

House of Balls
Minneapolis

In a big yellow brick building in the warehouse district on the edge of downtown there is a narrow shop window, into which is mounted a box with six push buttons; inside the window are strange skeletal figures, each with something set into motion by a different button. A finger moves, an arm, a head; a light goes on in the eyes. Over the door is a sign: HOUSE OF BALLS.

A violin finds itself in an uncomfortable situation.

The artist himself, dressed for dinner.

You open the shop door cautiously and find yourself in what could be a medieval craftsman's shop in a heavy wooden structure; muted colors, low lighting, and an incredible profusion of unfamiliar objects. The place is crammed with startling constructions. Life-sized transparent steel figures stand in various attitudes: One is welded entirely from drill bits. Percussive music comes from the next room, music you never hear on the radio, music of late-night bacchanalias, music of lost inhibitions. A wild-looking green-and-yellow human head seems to have been carved somewhere in the South American jungles by a lost culture.

On a stand you see another very human head made entirely of flatware, a startled look on its face that is somehow menacing and comic at the same time. There are other exotic heads, some on figures and some on platters, with eloquent eyes and expressive mouths, this one bizarre and vaguely threatening, that one with a great sense of peace, all rich in color and shaped from some indestructible colored stone, for all appearances more durable than marble, and you're told that they're carved from bowling balls.

You would never know it. Bowling balls are layered—like the planet—different in the core from the mantle. Carving into them in a flowing way creates unexpected and powerful color contrasts.

Al Christian says that the idea of the shop and gallery is to show that art doesn't come from waving a magic wand—you sit and you work at it, and it is a lot of work. He uses the same shaped drill bits they use on stone and a 6-inch flexible vacuum hose propped close to the work to draw off the hard plastic dust. He tells about the evolution of the bowling ball and why the older ones are better for carving, and which are the rarest and best.

His beater pickup is parked in the next block with HOUSE OF BALLS painted on the side. Bowling pins stand on the roof, like old milk jugs in cartons, and half pins decorate the sides.

The House of Balls is located at 212 3rd Avenue North and 2nd Street in the warehouse district of Minneapolis. The studio is open around midnight, by appointment, and Saturday noon to 4:00 P.M. Call (612) 332–3992 or see it on the Web at www.houseofballs.com.

SHE RODE WITH JOHN DILLINGER

*R*uby Rydeen grew up on a farm on County Road 3 in Washington County, about a mile from Big Marine Lake. The back pasture was forested and extended to the shoreline, and it was her daily chore, at the age of twelve, to go out there with her younger brother Leroy and bring in the cows. They were offered a ride one day by a man in a black pickup; she climbed in first and sat next to John Dillinger. He gave them each a sucker and she remembers that hers was the red one; she doesn't recall what color Leroy got. He let them out at the pasture gate and went on to his cabin on the lake. Ruby remembers Dillinger as a nice man.

It's long been an open secret that Chicago gangsters of the Prohibition era—a time now referred to as if it were a geologic period—had an understanding with the local cops and sheriffs that as long as they stayed straight in these parts they wouldn't be bothered. And it worked for a while, until a couple of intergang hits in 1933 upset the locals and they were forced to act.

Ruby remembers that the Dillinger cabin had about a dozen chickens in the yard. It wasn't that the boys couldn't afford eggs or that they were trying to fool the neighbors, because everybody knew what they were up to; it's just that chickens make pretty good lookouts, and you can't shut 'em up by tossing steak at them. He bought the chickens from Joseph Dahlquist, Ruby's great-uncle, and he also got his mail at Dahlquist's mailbox. Nobody wanted to know too much, and people tried hard not to see or hear anything. Her older brother Lawrence, wiser to the world than she, was reluctant to go out in the fields when "the boys" were around.

The Dillinger cabin has stood empty above the lake for twenty-five years, the chicken house leaning badly behind it. No one seems to know who owns the property, but rumor has it someone recently bought it. Folks are wondering if the historical society will want that chicken house restored to its former glory.

Take Washington County 3 to 177th Street, turn west onto Norell, then north onto 182nd. Turn left; the famous but modest buildings sit 300 feet west of the intersection.

WORLD'S TALLEST BICYCLE
Minneapolis

The Hard Times Bike Club is more a loose affiliation than a club: no meetings, no schedule, no dues, no membership manual. But of course you wouldn't call yourself the Hard Times Bike Loose Affiliation, so it's a club. They build and ride tall bikes but not the kind that one remembers seeing old pictures of, with the big wheel in front and the little one in back and no chain, variously called velocipedes, high wheels, or penny farthings. These tall bikes are built of an ordinary woman's bicycle frame welded on top of a man's frame, with a chain running from the upper sprocket position down to the rear wheel.

If you are a tall bike biker you will run alongside and push to get it going, and then in a quick and athletic move you will hop up to the horizontal tube of the lower frame—which is now the middle of the bike—and swing your other foot even higher, through the V up there at eye level, and start pedaling. If you don't have momentum and balance at this critical instant you will fall a fall that will be four times worse than your usual crash from a bicycle. If you should somehow maintain and find yourself in the miracle of street traffic and you later need to stop at a red light, you will make it over to the curb and hang on to the post until the light changes. And then you will have a new problem, starting from a dead stop that far in the air.

That's how it works for most tall bikes, anyway. The world's tallest bike is something else altogether, and in fact there is only one man allowed to even try to ride it, because it's 12 feet up to the seat and he has to lie flat to go under a freeway overpass. It was built by an artist and mechanic, a lean Swede named Per Hanson who is the club president, and it is ridden only by a gymnastic young man named Stranj. (There's a long *a* in that.) He rides it mostly in parades, given that it takes an entourage to get him up there and to bring it safely to a stop and get him back down.

The Hard Times Cafe, a West Bank co-op the city tried unsuccessfully to shut down, serves as the casual meeting ground for the club, but there are inner-city garages and backyards where most of the welding and mechanical work is done; a favorite junkyard yields up frames and chains and parts, some left by friends and supporters. The builders and riders are generally phoneless and footloose, some homeless, some with facial tattoos, body metal, and so forth; at a club get-together in an

Stranj, tall in the saddle and presumably heading for the Guinness Book of World Records.

art gallery they said some members held jousting contests from the high bikes using PVC pipe wrapped with foam. Four out of five of them could remember their grandmother's telephone number.

A college literature professor said about the Hard Times Cafe: "It is an authentic Parisian cafe of the 1920s; it's literary, it's intellectual, it's artistic and it also has real people, the poor and the homeless. People my age talk a lot about diversity; this place is diversity, and it threatens them."

All of which is probably true, but it also provides sustenance to the builders of the World's Tallest Bicycle.

The Hard Times Cafe is located at Riverside Avenue and Cedar Avenue on the West Bank in Minneapolis.

TIGER JACK

*H*e was born in New York, on Long Island, in 1907; his mother died when he was seven and he was sent to live with relatives near Danville, Virginia. He came to Minnesota during the Great Depression, as he used to say, "in a boxcar, with a tag on my ankle," which he later revealed was partly true and partly poetic license. He spent one night in a St. Paul mission and woke up the next day determined to become a boxer, so he went to a 7th Street gym and said he was a hotshot from Ohio who'd had so many fights he couldn't count 'em all. The going rate was two and three dollars a fight; his first one was in borrowed trunks and shoes. He said, "I throwed glove and throwed glove and throwed glove. In two weeks I'd whipped everyone in my weight." He came by his nom de guerre when the sheriff's brother told him after a good fight that he had been a tiger out there, and it stuck. For two years he shined shoes and made door-to-door sales in daylight and boxed at night.

He married his wife, Nurceal, in 1946, and in 1949 they opened a small variety store on Rondo and Farrington Street: Rondo was the main street of a thriving black commercial district in those days, home to the Blind Pig Cafe, the Busy Bee Grocery, Booker T's Restaurant, the Blue Moon, Baby Muriel's, the Love Tailor Shop, the Dew Drop, Walker Williams Pool Hall and Grocery. And Field's Drug Store, Coleman's Little Harlem Restaurant, the Square Deal Liquor Store. They were all swept away when Interstate 94 was shoved through in the mid-1960s, and Rondo became a frontage road named Concordia.

Tiger Jack Rosenbloom was the only businessman to survive in the neighborhood; he moved the shack to the high corner where Dale Street crosses the freeway and shined shoes and sold charcoal, kerosene, candy, and greeting cards. At Christmas, he said, "I got a black Jesus and a white Jesus; some folks want one and some want the other."

He became the most famous and most popular man in St. Paul, and he stayed that way for thirty years. He was quotable. He favored hard work and spoke against government handouts: "If Tiger Jack was mayor," he said, "it would be harder for one of these people to receive a dime than for a dead man to stand up and walk." Governor Rudy Perpich declared December 29, 1978, "Tiger Jack Day." He got an anniversary card from Hubert Humphrey. His son Lucky is the chairman of the Minnesota Black Republican Coalition.

A steadfast man becomes an institution.

He said, "I'm no yes man, no get-by man. No one uses Tiger Jack. Everything I say is truth and logic." A local reporter asked him on his ninetieth birthday how his health was; he said, "Like an alligator." He also told him: "Tiger's commandments. Put 'em down: Be true. Your word is your word. Respect your fellow man. Respect your license."

He had an ability to touch people through word and deed and he kept his life simple, never went into debt, preached hard work and honesty, and sent eight children to school on the profits from an 8- by 10-foot charcoal and shoeshine shack. In April of his ninety-fourth year the city named a street after him and his wife: "Mr. and Mrs. Tiger Jack Street." He died that August on the birthday of his daughter Mona, who had preceded him. He knew he would go that day; he said his good-byes and told people Mona would call him home, and so she did.

The family gave his shack on Dale and the freeway to the city; they say it's going to become a historic site.

Tiger's Shack has been moved to the Minnesota Historical Society at 345 West Kellogg Boulevard in St. Paul. The museum's hours are Tuesday 10:00 A.M. to 8:00 P.M., Wednesday through Saturday 10:00 A.M. to 5:00 P.M., and Sunday noon to 5:00 P.M. Call (651) 296–6126 for more information.

THE HOUSE OF MARI MAE
Minneapolis

P age 131 of *New Art International* says: "Exuberantly force-ful and brightly charismatic, the elaborate folk visions of Mari Mae Newman stretch their roots down through mythic lace of clouds to the raucous and sublime loam of contemporary culture. . . ." And it goes on from there. Maybe a bit overheated, but the accompanying prints of her paintings are really cool.

She had an art stand in their front yard when other kids were selling lemonade; at thirteen she had a solo show and at twenty-five sold a painting to a museum. Her work has been in the papers, on television, and in important collections, and she's established a national name for herself as a self-taught artist, a visionary in the field of what they call outsider or naive art. But she's not exactly uneducated: Her entry in *Who's Who in American Art* lists her as Newman, Mari Alice Mae, Painter, Sculptor, b. Esterville, Iowa, and reveals that she stud-ied at the University of Minnesota and the Minneapolis College of Art and Design and has certificates in cabinetry, upholstery, and jewelry making.

But, as she told a reporter, despite the media attention and getting her works into museums, she's had this problem: ". . . Been doing this since I was five years old, and I have yet to be able to make a living at it. . . ." Over the years she's worked as a dishwasher, parking lot attendant, in factories and meatpack-ing plants, at a hospital. In 1989 she decided to make her house into her résumé. She painted it as few houses have been painted before; it's become a city landmark in the last decade. Local citizens will direct you to the place.

And it fits all those adjectives the critics use: *colorful, bril-liant, vivid, humorous, quirky,* and so forth; the steps and side-walks are covered with moving rectangles of color, and there is an immense amount of detail in the panels on the front porch.

Mari Mae in front of her multicolored house. As they say in the want ads: "Must see to appreciate."

She changes them and sometimes presents images of nonspecific social commentary, which some take the wrong way, writing angry letters to the newspaper; she shrugs off the controversy. The yard is a landscape of bright-painted tree stumps and the occasional current sculpture, and the roof is entirely of alternating red and white shingles.

It looks like a house in a children's book of fairy tales. If we had a color spread here we could show it off a little, but, lacking that, if you get to Minneapolis you should take a swing by Mari's place. For a small donation she'll even give you a tour of the place; you will be amazed.

Mari Mae Newman's house is at 5117 Penn Avenue South in Minneapolis. Phone (612) 922–6439.

BLACK AND WHITE

He's known among artists and enthusiasts as Scott Seekins, but to the city in general he's the Black and White Guy; all black in winter, all white in summer. He has a severely angular appearance, exaggerated by machete sideburns and a thin slice of mustache, a weave of black curls, and large Buddy Holly glasses. In a white linen dinner jacket, white pants, black leather shoes, and a large art deco brooch, he is an eye-catching combination of elements; the artist as art.

He realized in high school that he didn't quite fit in, saying that in the 1960s he was the only person his age in South St. Paul who wasn't a hippie. He went on to art school in Min- neapolis and along the way developed an interest in turn-of- the-twentieth-century men's formal styles, eventually settling on seasonal black and white. He found a couple of antique cloth-

Scott Seekins sees the world in black and white.

ing stores on the bus routes between home and school and built a wardrobe fit for a high-tone gentleman of another age. He says, "If you just stand still, you'll be back in style sometime."

He's been hollered at a lot over the years, as in: "Ya look like ya got a cat on yer head, ya [drive-by vulgarity]!" About that, he says, "Conformity is strong in the suburb of Sweden. Each group polarizes into itself and is fearful of the others. . . . They accept you, but they don't. It hurts you in all kinds of ways, relationships, all kinds of things. I'm not a good person to bring home to Mama . . . because of the look. Three times, when I've been going with somebody and then we meet her parents, they take one look at me and they say to their daughter: 'Where have we gone wrong?' Three times! 'Where have we gone wrong?' And in each case, it was over. The girls say it's just too much pressure, they can't handle it. It's way too hard. . . ."

He developed a focus on painting Madonnas in contemporary settings, often with local historical landmarks over their shoulder and often with himself hidden in the background. He's done 1,000 paintings of the Madonna in the last fifteen years, "more than were done in the Renaissance. I just felt one day that it was a positive image. It's not so much a Catholic thing." He's an expert model railroad detailer, president of the Twin Cities N-Scalers club, and writes articles in the various hobby publications. His interest in early rock, rockabilly, and R&B has landed him guest disc jockey spots on local radio, and he collects reptiles and will bring them to local schools and give talks. He's also a historian, a specialist in World War II, and a fly fisherman. That rarest of Minnesotans, a man without a car, he carries a fly rod on the bus to city lakes.

But it's the outfit, and the big dry-cleaning bills that go with it, that has made him into the city's harbinger of the seasons: Winter ends when Scott changes to his whites, and he alone makes the decision, based strictly on his instincts. Two seasons here: Black and White. And he'll let you know.

Scott's studio is located above Nate's Clothing on 1st Avenue North and 3rd Street in the warehouse district of Minneapolis.

CORK TRUCK
Minneapolis

Houston is generally recognized as the Capital City of the Art
Car and most people are okay with that; it is, after all, the
Metro Petro. And while it may stage the world's largest art car
parade, it's not the only parade, and a determined lady in Minneapolis is seeing to it that her city gets its just due; she is not
only an artist but also a street museum curator. She has set the
standard here with her 1980 Mazda pickup crawling with
10,000 wine-bottle corks, acquired in thirteen years of working
in an Italian restaurant. Set in adhesive, generally end-to-end
in flowing rows, they give the vehicle a tan corduroy look,
inset with a reverse CORK TRUCK across the front bumper and an
ART CAR across the tailgate. And a circular design on the hood
and other artistic touches that are better seen than described.

Which is the case with most art, of course, but the art critic
business is a huge industry that requires no proficiency test or
license and, well, we thought, why not have a modest go at it
ourselves? Seems the only way to tell if a new style is real art or
not is whether or not it seems goofy to the general public. If
something comes along that everybody likes right away, then it's
not art; but if a few folks really go nuts for it and almost everyone else says why bother, then it's most likely art. And if there's
a sense of humor in there somewhere, then it's art for sure.

And these art cars in the parade here that Jan Elftmann
organizes, and in the few others around the country, these definitely meet the criteria. Jan herself meets the criteria: She has
a fine dress made of wine corks, and she has covered a bowling
alley entirely in wine corks—balls, pins, and alley. She has siz-
able forearms from years of squeezing an adhesive gun. And of ·
course every wine cork has a story, so her old beater pickup is

Jan Elftmann and her 10,000-story pickup truck.

carrying an unlikely blend of 10,000 dinners, meetings, parties, and trysts, glued end-to-end and side-by-side and driving
around town.

Other vehicles seen in Minneapolis parades: a Surfin' Car
covered with seashells and featuring two beautiful women's
heads on the front fenders with seashells for hair; the Bone
Car, covered with real bones—but no human ones, a question
folks ask her all the time; Miss Vicki, the tulip car designed for
Tiny Tim; a truck shingled with pages from James Joyce; the
Trophy Car, bearing 150 trophies and awards; a '75 Caddie in
the form of a leaping orange horse with a papier-mâché head
and legs and a rope tail.

Wild alterations to ordinary vehicles—like the 13-foot-tall tail fins on a Houston car named Max the Daredevil Finmobile—seldom seem to add anything to the trade-in value; the upside is that, as art car pioneer Ruthann Godelleri put it, "Unlike galleries and museums, art cars are open twenty-four hours a day, and they're free."

The Art Car Parade can be seen on the Fourth of July as part of the Greenway Parade of Arts in Minneapolis. It starts at 1:00 P.M. on Lyndale and follows Lake Street to 5th Street. It is organized by Intermedia Arts; call (612) 871–4444 or visit the Web site at www.intermediaarts.org.

TWELVE-LEVEL TREE HOUSE
St. Louis Park

It began back in Springfield, Virginia, when Mark Tucker was a little kid and a tree house behind the family home was taken down by a bulldozer to make room for a school. He never got that tree house thing out of his system. He married a Minnesota woman, they moved here, he built up a business, they had five kids, and all along he meant to build a tree house in the big spreading maple in the yard. When the oldest was sixteen and moved out of the house, Mark realized he should have built that tree house and he'd better get to it soon, before any more left. He put his insurance business on hold and went down to the lumberyard.

And once he started he couldn't stop; he had six levels up there in the first year and his kids thought it was great. He had a grand opening and invited folks up there and in the next few years got the notion to put his office there—called it his branch office, of course—and pretty soon the city was on his case. They wanted handrails and regulation stairs and structural engineers and load limits and reports from foresters and he didn't, and he kept adding levels and additions and pretty soon the city was threatening to tear the whole thing down, all twelve levels of it. And, like so many of our wild romantic notions and obsessive-impulsive constructions, it became fodder for lawyers.

The court settlement allowed him to have family members plus four up there at any one time, and it has to undergo annual inspections and special inspections after storms and a whole invoice of other governmental mothering—that he has to pay for—but they are letting it stay there. He says it's a good place for the kids and for him to get away and watch TV or read. There were times he wished he'd never built it, but now he's thinking it's pretty cool.

And for all of that, it is an amazing thing to see. As wide as it is tall, it emerges from the ground part mushroom, part pirate ship, and part precarious Gothic castle; it looks like an illustration in a children's story book. It intertwines in the branches, platforms wrapping around the trunk here and decks spreading out onto large branches over there, all very organic. Once up into the main forks of the branches, it climbs 40 feet farther into the crown of the big tree, where there is a high observation post and you can see for at least a couple of miles, anyway. They say it creaks in a windstorm like a wooden sailing ship.

The tree house is located at 4800 Minnetonka Boulevard in St. Louis Park. To get there take Minnetonka Boulevard east off Minnesota Highway 100 for a few blocks. It's on the left side of the road. For information about tours call Mark Tucker at (952) 920–6627.

Drop the Broom and Call the Bat Abaters

*T*o them, abatement *means "rescue," not "extermination." It began when Mickey went to a seminar about bats at the university, where she learned that some fruit bats have wingspans of 6 feet and some live to be thirty years old; she became enamored of the domestic qualities and usefulness of bats in general. She had cause to rescue a few and kept them, and she and her husband, Greg, became known as the Bat Abaters, people you could call if you were freaked out by bats in your house. They got rabies prevention shots and became registered with the DNR, and they found their spare room gradually filling with bats in various states of rehabilitation.*

It's not a full-time occupation. They get about fifty calls a year, from people like the woman who called of a recent morning from a cell phone: they found her sitting in her driveway in her car with the windows up, holding a tennis racket in a very tight grip. She was barefoot, wearing a shower cap and a raincoat over her pajamas, and she was what they used to call "nervous." Nervous is kind of an understatement, and it's not an unfamiliar scene to them. They did a thorough search of the house and found no bat, finally leaving her to her private terror there with a harmless furry little mammal. He never did come back but the woman had an uneasy time of it for a while, despite their soothing assurances as to the gentle ways of the bat community.

There are nearly 1,000 species, about a quarter of all the known families of mammals. Most eat flying insects, but in the Tropics their tastes run to all kinds of bugs, frogs, pollen—without bats there wouldn't be tequila, because they pollinate the agave plant—and a lot of them go for ripe fruit in the rain forests.

We don't have much in the way of overripe fruit here, but Minnesota's state bird is said to be the mosquito and we're blessed with a great abundance of them, so that's the kind of bats we have. The brown bats are the speedy little guys; you see them in late evening doing silent aerial acrobatics in the far corner of the yard. Down in the lower latitudes of Texas a place called the Bracken Cave is home to 20 million Mexican free-tail bats; they go out every night and eat 200 tons of insects. Doing the math, it means each bat eats 0.02 pound of bugs, which is about the weight of two teaspoons of water. To find all these bugs they'll climb to 10,000 feet and catch winds and travel long distances. Our bats don't have to go to that much trouble; the state birds are not that hard to find here.

There is also a place in Texas where one can take nonreleasable bats; a woman down there runs a homeless bat shelter, and Greg and Mickey finally took theirs down to her when they became too much to deal with at home. Kind of like dumping the kids off at college.

Anyway, they have become so good at what they do they've become known as Master Bat Abaters.

For fascinating bat information call Greg and Mickey Froehle at (612) 926–2882 or visit www.bat conservationinternational.com.

PAVEK MUSEUM OF BROADCASTING
St. Louis Park

In 1927 you could buy a new Model A Ford for $585. An Amberola radio cost $600. You not only couldn't get the radio in the car, but if you got the radio you couldn't afford the car. In small towns it was not uncommon to find only one radio in the whole community, and if the owner was generous he would put it in the window and let his neighbors listen.

By 1927 Joe Pavek was nineteen years old and it had already been nine years since he built his first radio, which was struck by lightning, burst into flames, and set fire to his mother's curtains, which caused his mother to throw the radio out the window. Joe went on to become a radio repairman, a bookkeeper, a sales manager, and a paint distributor, but he's well known these days because of his fabulous collection of old radios and broadcasting equipment. He started this museum in 1988 and died in 1989; it has been augmented by the Charles Bradley Collection and the Jack Mullin Collection, so that it's now the second largest museum of its type in the world.

They have 12,000 square feet of stuff there you never imagined: a big 1912 rotary spark-gap transmitter like the one used on the *Titanic* to transmit distress signals; an 1896 wireless device invented by Guglielmo Marconi himself; a 1903 Zonophone gramophone; the 1912 Edison Amberola; Airtones, Operadios, Magnadynes, Atwater-Kents. There's the Grunow twelve-tube Teledial, the RCA Radiola Super Hetrodyne, the Kennedy Coronet, and the Grebe Synchrophase, whose motto was "Get It Better with a Grebe."

And they have the unbelievable RCA Theremin, the only musical instrument ever made that you didn't touch to play. It's in a small desklike cabinet containing a speaker and sprouting

"How many times do I have to tell you kids to turn that thing down?"

two antennae, one vertical for pitch and one horizontal for volume; as your hand moves along the antenna it wails and moans, rising and falling, loud and soft. The sales brochure says: ". . . Yet, WE . . . ALL . . . YOU . . . can now play, and play beautifully, a wonderfully expressive, marvelously simple, absolutely unmechanical musical instrument! Scientists and musicians of note and of standing have gone on record with their opinions that the Theremin may likely revolutionize the whole world of music. . . ." It never happened. The thing wails like a saw.

Joe was about ready to auction off the amazing collection in 1984 when the inventor of the wearable pacemaker, Earl Bakken—the cofounder of Medtronic and a radio junkie himself—stepped up and helped form the museum, which he saw as a great opportunity for education. It opened on the fiftieth anniversary of Orson Welles's *War of the Worlds* broadcast, and although the public is welcome, it functions primarily as an educational museum for grade school children. It's booked solid every year; they've done 1,600 workshops for more than 30,000 kids since 1991.

It is one of the five best-kept secrets in Minnesota, or at least it was until this book got published.

The Pavek Museum of Broadcasting is located at 3515 Raleigh Avenue in St. Louis Park. To get there take Minnesota Highway 100 south, go east on Route 25, then right on Beltline Road to Raleigh Street. Call about tours at (952) 926–8198.

I G U A N A

S t . P a u l

A remarkable steel sculpture lies on the lower entrance plaza to the Science Museum of Minnesota: a 3,900-pound, 40-foot lizard, lifelike, poised as if ready to make a sudden move on any approaching meaty object, such as yourself; you find yourself comforted by the fact that you might be quicker than some of the people around you.

He was welded together of 13,000 railroad spikes, the head of each spike a single scale on his extraordinary hide, by an artist named Nick Swearer, from Northfield. (Anyone who has ever worked on a section gang would appreciate an artist working with rail spikes having the name *Swearer*.) Nick

A lizard beyond your expectations.

began it when he was fifteen, using his own iguana as a model, and it took four years to finish, working every day after school; art patrons Betty and John Musser paid him $10,000 for it and donated it to the museum. The beast has been a great favorite in this city for twenty-one years.

When the museum made ready to move to their new building in 1999 they threw a big party for Iggy, as he's called, and then a few days later hoisted him onto a flatbed trailer and paraded him through crowds in downtown Minneapolis and St. Paul to his new spot near the river.

A huge iguana welded of rail spikes. Amazing such a rough concept could turn out to be such a tour de force; so graceful and so appealing. Kids climb all over him. His snout is smooth from people patting it as they pass. Nick told the newspaper he never oiled it; "He is oiled by human oil, and he would be a red rust if he were not touched so much . . . it shows how much people love him."

The Science Museum of Minnesota is located at 120 West Kellogg Boulevard, across from RiverCentre in downtown St. Paul. Museum hours are Monday through Wednesday 9:30 A.M. to 5:30 P.M., Thursday through Saturday 9:30 A.M. to 9:00 P.M., and Sunday 10:30 A.M. to 5:30 P.M. Call (651) 221-9444 or visit www.smm.org for information.

THE MUSEUM OF QUESTIONABLE MEDICAL DEVICES
St. Paul

Bob McCoy is president of the Minnesota Skeptics, who post a standing offer of $10,000 to anyone who can furnish solid evidence supporting the existence of ghosts, but he is better known as the curator of the nation's largest museum of quackery gear. It began in 1983 when he and a friend salvaged twelve phrenology machines from the 1920s and started a phrenology parlor in a shopping mall. The machines look like outsized hooded hair dryers; for a modest few dollars they'd read your cranial lumps and tell you things about yourself— your intelligence, spirituality, chastity, suavity, wit, ideality, and twenty-nine other qualities—and if you weren't pleased with how you tested out Bob said he could rearrange your lumps: "I have a mallet handy."

The phrenology machine—precursor to the Minnesota
Multiphasic Personality Test.

He began acquiring other wacky machines from garage
sales and other collectors, and from places like the defunct St.
Louis Medical Quackery Museum. The collection has grown to
325 unique and interesting ways for a person to make a complete fool of himself, or herself. There's soap that sudses off
your extra pounds, and weight reduction glasses that you wear
standing in front of lights flashing prismatic colors in your

face. He has the 1918 G-H-R Electric Thermitis Dilator, which is a rectally inserted electric "prostate warmer" that plugs into a wall outlet and stimulates the male "abdominal brain"; the foot-operated breast-enlarging Nemectron Machine, a pump that attaches to the kitchen sink and allows a lady to enlarge her bust while she washes the dishes. (Fellas: a real thoughtful gift for that special gal.)

The Crosley Xervac is a vacuum-powered hair restorer; the Spectro-Chrome machine, invented in 1920 by one Dinshah P. Ghaliali, could cure patients of almost any malady through the proper use of pure and intense colored light, broken down from sunlight. William Reich's 1940 invention, called the Orgone Energy Accumulator, is a "storehouse of orgasmic energy," an ordinary box of fiberboard and steel wool with a galvanized metal lining; sit in there for the prescribed thirty minutes and . . . wow. You've just sat in a box for a while.

The turn of the twentieth century brought on a burst of actual scientific progress, which fueled a huge market for charlatans, including those pushing things like radium water. Few people knew that Madame Curie, one of the pioneers in research on radioactivity, had her fingers fall off before she died; a captain of the steel industry, Eben MacBurney Byers, boasted that he had drunk 1,400 bottles of radium water in two years. He died in 1930 after his jaw fell off.

But flummery didn't disappear in the 1930s—in the 1960s the Ruth Drown radio therapy machine enticed thousands to have their saliva analyzed while it emitted healing rays. In 1995 the FDA seized a "radio" machine from a health store that claimed it could cure AIDS; it was nothing more than a plastic box with knobs. Holistic magazines are still full of this stuff: For thirty-nine dollars plus S&H you can get an electric pain relief zapper, the same item that's called a barbecue grill spark igniter and available for less than ten bucks at a chain store.

Bob McCoy is now semi-retired, and his fabulous and famous collection has been moved to the Collections Room at the Science Museum of Minnesota, where it is a big hit.

The museum is located at 120 West Kellogg Boulevard, across from RiverCentre in downtown St. Paul. Museum hours are Monday through Wednesday 9:30 A.M. to 5:30 P.M., Thursday through Saturday 9:30 A.M. to 9:00 P.M., and Sunday 10:30 A.M. to 5:30 P.M. Call (651) 221–9444 or visit www.smm.org for more information.

MICKEY'S DINER
St. Paul

One of the few businesses in the metro area that has remained unchanged through the last forty years, Mickey's is one of those things—like the violin, for instance—that they got right early on and so why fool with it.

It's had close calls, the closest just a few years back when they expanded the St. Paul Companies insurance headquarters, but after the dust settled there it still sat, on a skinny strip of land at the corner of St. Peter and 7th, its back up against a gigantic new masonry wall; it has art deco attitude there in its resolute cream-and-red railroad car getup. It looks like that wall will come down before Mickey's leaves.

And it could happen that way because Mickey's was hauled in from New Jersey in 1938 and is on the National Register of Historic Places, one of only two diners in the nation so honored. It's been in four movies and quite a few notables have sat there; we could start dropping names but we won't. But it's as much theater as it is restaurant—and, as one of the few places left to stay open twenty-four hours, as much necessity as luxury. If you need a breakfast suggestion, a lot of us go for the Twos: two eggs, two sausage, two cakes. For dinner, the Mulligan stew or the half-pound hamburger steak, with onions. Soup of the day is ham and bean, every day. The coffee mugs

Mickey's motto: "You are what you eat—Be all you can be."

are like the building itself: sturdy and exactly right for the purpose. So is the coffee.

The waitresses are generally feisty and don't put up with a lot of nonsense; they'll tell you to get a job if they figure you're unemployed out of sheer laziness. If you're tipsy and out of line they'll tell you to behave. One is from Wisconsin, a Packer fan, and she says she doesn't give a rip about the Vikings and that they've never amounted to anything anyways, and when a regular customer said she should be careful not to say that too loud in there, she threw her good-sized shoulders back and said: "I don't care if they don't like it. Bring 'em on. C'mon! Get a shiner at Mickey's Diner! Haha!"

Mickey's Diner is located at 36 West 7th Street and Cedar Avenue in downtown St. Paul. It's always open. For more information call (651) 222-5633.

YOU CAN'T ALWAYS GET WHAT YOU WANT

*I*n 1964 the Rolling Stones made their first tour of the United States; one of the stops on the way was at Danceland, a ballroom out on Lake Excelsior, west of the Twin Cities. The gig didn't really go that well and the band was actually booed, which may have said more about the crowd than the band, depending on your viewpoint.

There is a man in the nearby small town of Excelsior named Jimmy, sometimes referred to as Mister Jimmy, who has been there as long as almost anyone can remember. He lives with his brother and walks around town, often chewing on an unlit cigar, checking things out, talking to people. He lights the Christmas lights on the main street; he's sort of the honorary town ambassador. He may or may not have an occupation, but that's not relevant to the story. What is relevant is that on the morning after the Stones gig at Danceland, Jimmy was in the Beacon Drug Store, apparently minding the counter for a few minutes, when Mick Jagger walked in. He ordered a cherry Coke and said he was looking for some item and Jimmy took it upon himself to help, not knowing who he was dealing with at the time and who would have, back then?

They searched the shelves for whatever it was Mick was seeking without success but were finally able to come up with something else that would probably work just as well, and in fact, maybe even better. As Mick was paying for it, Jimmy made the offhand comment that "I guess you can't always get what you want, but if you try, sometimes you can get what you need."

In the song he wrote from that remark, You Can't Always Get What You Want, *Jagger has changed the Beacon to the Chelsea and altered the exchange somewhat, but he left Jimmy's name the same. It is now an unbelievable thirty-eight years later and neither one has undergone a career change.*

You can probably find Jimmy somewhere on the streets of Excelsior and Mick somewhere with the Rolling Stones. And if you can't find either one maybe you'll find what you need.

FOOD ON A STICK
Minnesota State Fair, St. Paul

I t is the largest state fair in the country and it features most of the things that any of the other fairs feature, including hogs the size of full-grown steers, steers up there at a ton, heavy as bison, and pumpkins the size of easy chairs. The puke-inducing rides, the sling-shot launching folks up into the goose fly-ways, the ring-the-bell mallets, darts and bal-loons, floating ducks, and all the rest. National rock and country acts in the grand-stand, stages all up and down the midway, people carrying huge stuffed animals.

The undisputed grand patriarch of stick food.

What really separates this fair from a lot of the others, however, is that, for ten days at the end of summer, it is likely the
world's largest market for boiling oil and sharp sticks. There is
an incredible array of food offered on a stick here, thirty-seven
varieties at last count, including Deep Fried Candy Bars,
Cheese on a Stick, Chocolate Covered Cheese, Chocolate Covered
Bananas, five kinds of Pickles on Sticks, the Field and Stream
(walleye and prime rib), Pizza on a Stick, Scotch Eggs, Teriyaki
Ostrich, and Alligator—either breaded or as Naked Alligator on
a Stick. And to cleanse the palate for some stick-mounted
Fudge Puppies and Taffy Pops, try Watermelon on a Stick.

Probably a good thing for all of us that the fair only comes
once a year; and that, at least so far, we have no chains of
boiled-in-oil food-on-a-stick restaurants either.

The Minnesota State Fair runs for the last ten days of summer,
including Labor Day. The fairgounds are located on Snelling
Avenue and Como Avenue north of Interstate 94 in St. Paul.

THE HOUSE OF SANTAS
Stillwater

It's a big English Tudor house of a mint-green color on the
corner of Wilkins and Owens; in the yard stands a 15-foot
Santa, alongside you-know-who the you-know-what-nosed rein-
deer. And even fully aware that you are about to enter a place
with twenty-one rooms holding 6,000 Santas, it still isn't something you're ready for.

You enter a scene that feels uneasily like you are in a
movie—not just on the set but in the movie already, and you
aren't quite sure it's Disney; it might be Quentin Tarantino.
Feels like anything could happen here. And they do come to

Dick and Lois with 6,000 fat guys in red overcoats.

life; a pair of life-sized fellows flanking the couch bend at the waist, raise an arm, and turn to the right a couple of times. A dance line on the mantel starts singing and doing the hula as they are turned on, a cacophony of Clauses. Others come to life with a clap of the hands, singing and yo-ho-hoing. There are international, political, and occupational Santas, cowboys and sailors and photographers. A glass case of biker Santas, on Harleys, naturally, and a pink bathroom full of pink Santas. A black Santa playing "Jingle Bell Rock" on a saxophone; a talking Vincent Price Santa. There is a Santa from Germany that is a hundred years old. You cannot find a corner anywhere to rest the eye without it falling on a Santa Claus; they are there in every size from half an inch tall on up, and they are there in incredible profusion.

The lady in charge of all this is Lois Kohns, a disarming person who likes to smile; she is married to exactly the right guy for this, Dick, who not only helps with the collecting and displays but also has a repair shop in the garage where he rebuilds the rough old antiques that come in. The menacing aspect of the scene melts away as she talks, not only of all the Santas but all the rest of it: the globe that says MERRY CHRISTMAS in whatever country's language you touch; the White House presidential ornaments; how it takes them two months to get ready for the Christmas tourists. Thousands of them, these days.

There is a room in the house where there are no Santas; it's the daughter's bedroom, upstairs, and it's an ordinary bedroom except maybe for her 1,000 Barbie dolls, all in the original boxes. Dick says, "This stuff keeps us going, keeps us excited about life. The worst thing I can think of is sitting in front of a television, doing nothing, waiting to die."

You leave marveling at the reach of the human imagination, to recast a fat white guy with white hair and whiskers into so many different incarnations. You wonder what future archaeologists would think if these were the only remnants of us found half a million years hence: "They had computers, but they worshipped fat guys in thick overcoats, looks like. One might have expected something more sophisticated."

The House of Santas is located at 1020 North Owens Street in Stillwater. Tours are available from Thanksgiving to January 15. For tour information call (651) 439–6110 or (651) 439–0066. There is an admission fee.

BUTTER SCULPTURES

If you drink milk and use dairy products and your father is a Minnesota dairy farmer or you have close ties to the dairy industry, and you are a reasonably attractive unmarried female high school graduate under the age of twenty-four, you are eligible to become a candidate for the title of Princess Kay of the Milky Way; statistically, you are more likely to be eligible to train as a navy fighter pilot and fly an F-18 Hornet than to become Princess Kay.

There are eleven dairy regions in the state and each sends a candidate to the state fair; one becomes princess and the rest are her court, but each is given a golden day in the sun, metaphorically, when her likeness is sculpted in butter. An artist named Linda Christensen starts with an eighty-five-pound block of it, 18 by 18 by 24 inches, and with knives and wooden paddles of varying sizes and small wire loops removes all the butter that doesn't look like the young lady.

The sitting takes place at thirty-eight degrees Fahrenheit, with the two of them on a revolving turntable inside a glass-walled cooler at the state fair. They are dressed in parkas and scarves and insulated boots, sometimes with three or four shirts, while huge crowds of people stand outside in the blazing heat and watch. The process takes six to eight hours. One model said, "We take an hour break for lunch, and we take a break every hour and a half or whenever the sculptor's nose starts running." It is one of the five main attractions at the fair, proving that Minnesotans do indeed know how to have a good time, regardless of what you may have heard.

The young women get to keep their likenesses, which contain roughly 192,000 calories; some give them to local pancake dinners and corn roasts and others save them for centerpieces at their wedding. One has kept her bust in a plastic bag in her freezer since 1980 and another cut just the face off and kept that in the freezer; every time she lifted the lid there she was, looking up at herself.

Ms. Christensen has had this part-time job since 1972, when she was a student at the Minneapolis College of Art

She's big, she's beautiful, and she's all butter.

and Design. As of September 2001 she had done 331 beauty queen butters, as well as a life-sized Elvis, Dolly Parton, and Michael Jackson for the Mid-South Fair in Memphis.

Butter sculpting used to be more common. Teddy Roosevelt made the famous "walk softly and carry a big stick" speech here at the Minnesota State Fair in 1901. When he returned in 1910, a local dairy had done a life-sized statue of him in butter wearing a pith helmet, his foot on the neck of a lion. (Did they think he meant a big stick of butter?)

You can watch Linda sculpt the princesses in the Empire Building at the Minnesota State Fair, which runs for the last ten days of summer, including Labor Day. The fairgrounds are located on Snelling Avenue and Como Avenue north of Interstate 94 in St. Paul. Call the Midwest Dairy Association at (651) 488–0261 for information.

FRANCONIA SCULPTURE PARK
Taylors Falls

It's both sculpture garden and workshop, open year-round and free to the public. It sits on sixteen acres of what was grazing land, on the west bluffs of the St. Croix River, a long-grass field bracketed by woods, with strange and dramatic objects spotted around. The materials and textures are generally the same as you would see on a neighboring abandoned farm: wood, rusting steel, stone, concrete. Occasional plaster on chicken wire, and some fiberglass. Colorful surfaces here and there and some surprises, like the elephant of steel reinforcing rods dancing on a welded steel ball, or the 40-foot-tall roller coaster.

They are produced by artists mostly from Minnesota and New York but also from South Carolina, Louisiana, Oregon, plus the United Kingdom, Colombia, Peru, and the Czech Republic; more than sixty-five pieces, with titles such as *Strange Time for a Blue Dance, Cephalopod, All Being Born 2 Seven, French Castings, Are You Down?, Heartburn.* And *Gorky's Pillow, Landing on Eros, Trunnion II, Chemical Calculations.* A large wooden wave rises over the grass, 20 feet high and 76 feet long, built by a man from Minneapolis.

Artists and interns come here to work and to learn, supported mostly by grants and donations. The founder and manager is sculptor John Hock. He says, "We don't have a set ideology. We just want to support anyone who wants to work in any medium. The crazier the better." But with most of the materials donated by local junkyards, machine shops, lumberyards, and quarries, or salvaged from construction sites, there emerges a certain rough continuity. And working with all this

Three Spheres *by Barbara Andrus.*

weight is as much common labor as it is artistic vision. Outdoor art in Minnesota is art that has been suffered for, and art that will itself suffer, sitting out there in the ice and cold and the lightning strikes. This place would make a good setting for a movie, especially one with big lightning strikes.

Franconia Sculpture Park is on U.S. Highway 8 at 29815 Unity Avenue, Shafer, Minnesota, about 2 miles west of Taylors Fall. It is free and open to the public every day year-round. Call (651) 465–3701 or visit www.info@franconia.org for more information.

MUMMY WITHOUT A VISA

*H*e's very compelling; lying there, mottled dark brown, looking like he's made of solidified dirt—which of course we all are—with large eyes closed and a head that seems too big for the skinny body. He's in a glass case in a gray-painted room; an explanation titled MUMMIFICATION hangs on the wall alongside an X ray of the guy. He's lying on his back in the bottom half of a sarcophagus; kids are leaning on the case. He is infinitely still; he moved 3,500 years ago and hasn't moved since.

This guy could never imagine he would someday be lying in a glass case with seasons of schoolchildren parading past, pointing and making comments. If you could go back in time and tell him that he would someday rest in a big museum and his picture would be on the Internet, he'd never believe you.

For a city to have a mummy was kind of a mark of the big leagues back around 1925, kind of like a symphony orchestra, or gangsters. The tomb of King Tutankhamen had been opened in 1922 and the Egyptian craze was in full force; and the St. Paul Institute, which is now the Science Museum of Minnesota, didn't have a mummy. A sixty-six-year-old lawyer named Simon Percy Crosby volunteered to go see if he could find one, and he did. Nobody knows where or how he bought it or how much he had to pay for it, which makes one suspect that Mr. Crosby was probably a pretty good lawyer. He shipped it back to himself and donated it to the institute.

It was in its mummy wrap but the hard-shell case didn't come with it, so they had a craftsman build the sarcophagus; it was painted as sort of a modern take on the Egyptian motif—modern in those days being art deco. They had no idea who this mummy was or what he did for a living or even where he was found.

So for a while they had it on display but not right out there where you'd see it, and they had a small plaque, mounted low, explaining that the fellow hadn't come with a pedigree. The museum staff eventually got to work and found the brain had been removed, which dated it to the later years of mummification, and they concluded the guy's head was shaved and he did a lot of barefoot walking but not much manual labor. There were other clues as well, and they were able to establish he'd been a priest, maybe thirty-five years old.

So they moved it out into the more public areas and it was a big hit, and stayed that way when they moved from the auditorium into a mansion and then into their own building. Now it's in the spanking-new downtown quarters overlooking the Mississippi, and some aren't that crazy about having a dead guy around for people to gawk at, so it's in a special exhibit about the history of the museum. Sort of a "we used to do it this way but we don't anymore" kind of setting, like an exhibit of plowing with oxen, only it's about we used put dead people out there to look at but we don't do it now. But we do have to admit it's sort of fascinating.

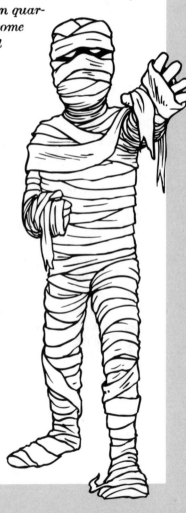

The mummy can be found in the Collections Room of the Science Museum of Minnesota, which is located at 120 West Kellogg Boulevard across from RiverCentre in downtown St. Paul. Museum hours are Monday through Wednesday 9:30 A.M. to 5:30 P.M., Thursday through Saturday 9:30 A.M. to 9:00 P.M., and Sunday 10:30 A.M. to 5:30 P.M. Call (651) 221–9444 or visit www.smm.org for more information.

WIENER DOG HURDLES
Wayzata

For many of us the essence of high-tone humor lies in the perverse staging of contests wherein even the winner will end up looking foolish, like three-legged racing or blueberry pie eating—contests for which the entrants are unlikely to possess any inner grace or aptitude. We wouldn't say a search for foolishness was the driving force behind the establishment of the annual wiener dog hurdles in Wayzata. But it's likely.

They've been going on for twelve years or so and there are now upward of sixty dogs entered; too many beasts to run all at once, so they stage heats, five racers per heat. The Miniature Dachshunds run with the regular full-sized Dachshunds and they all wear little capes, like silks on thoroughbreds, with their numbers on them. It's a grass course with a starting gate but no lane markings, about 30 yards long, with three short hurdles crossing the field at measured intervals. A short hurdle is one a Dachshund can't crawl under and can barely jump over; a 4-inch hurdle. There is also a Couch Jump, on the same course but with a small couch across the track; and the Leap into the Chair, a timed event wherein the owner sits in a chair some distance from the gate and the dog is released, runs, and leaps into his lap. And for the purists who crave sheer speed, there is the straight-ahead full-bore Sprint Race with no leaping involved.

Parents generally handle the dogs at the gate and children call to them from the finish line. The gates open, the announcer says, "AND THEY'RE OFF!" and all pandemonium breaks loose; kids shrieking, parents yelling, dogs barking and running all over. They get to that first hurdle and some leap right over and others stop dead, and yet others go running around the end, which is to say off the track. They don't get docked for this, but the dog who end-arounds the hurdles will seldom be later seen in the winners' circle—except in one recent race when all five dogs ran around all three hurdles. At the Leap into the Chair event a lot of dogs who have been trained to stay off the furniture come busting out of the gate and then skid to a stop at the chair, unable, literally, to make the leap. These same dogs often have trouble with the Couch Hurdle.

You wouldn't buy a wiener dog to run down antelope. They all discovered eons ago that they liked the sound of human laughter better than they liked the taste of antelope meat, and they set their genetic code to that course. And once a year, here beside an ancient glacial lake, their deepest primeval dreams come true as their owners and people they don't even know laugh until they are nearly sick.

The dogs race as part of James J. Hill Days in Wayzata. Call the chamber of commerce at (952) 473–9595 for race times, or visit www.wayzatachamber.com.

INDEX

ABOUT THE AUTHORS

Denise Remick was raised in St. Paul's storied East Side. She hopped a westbound freight train to Seattle on a summer break from college and has followed an abiding interest in people and places ever since, once leading a horse expedition from Minnesota to Colorado (they didn't quite make it). She has worked as a cartographer and is currently employed as a production artist in a Minneapolis ad agency. She is the daughter of the lady who rode with John Dillinger.

Russ Ringsak was raised in Grafton, North Dakota, back in the good old days when snowdrifts reached second-story windows. He was a registered architect in Minnesota when he bought an over-the-road semi tractor in 1977, a career move that ultimately led him to driving trucks and writing for the *Prairie Home Companion* radio show. His great-grandfather owned the *Rosebud*, the steamboat upon which Mark Twain was once employed.